The Bag of Scribbles

By RL Lane

Introduction: "It looks like a scribble", she said. Oh. I am supposed to make a book of scribbles. It will only have my scribble drawings...

Dedicated to my Dad. He probably gave me that crayon to draw my first scribble.

The first scribble drawing I ever did as an author was of an owl. I called it the "scribble screech owl". He lived…loved owls. My Dad loved owls when he lived…

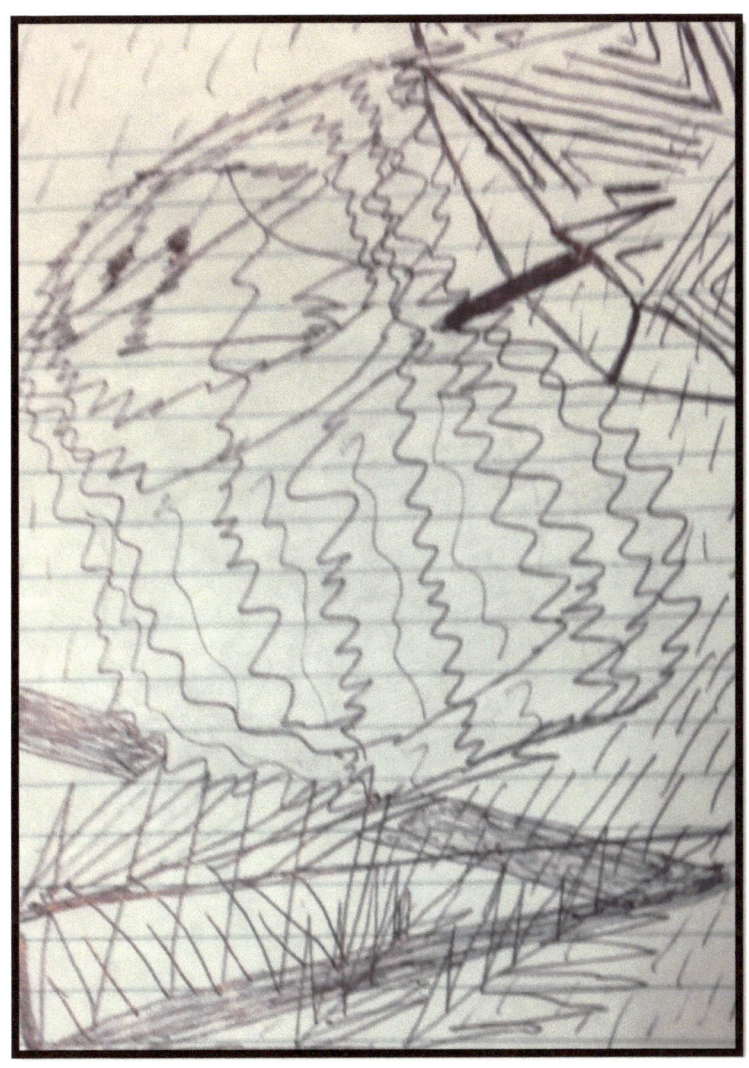

"Scribble Screech Owl"

Screen screen…screech screech is the sound it makes

Screech screech on the screen

Of life

He sits and watches

Looks all around

Then takes another look

All around

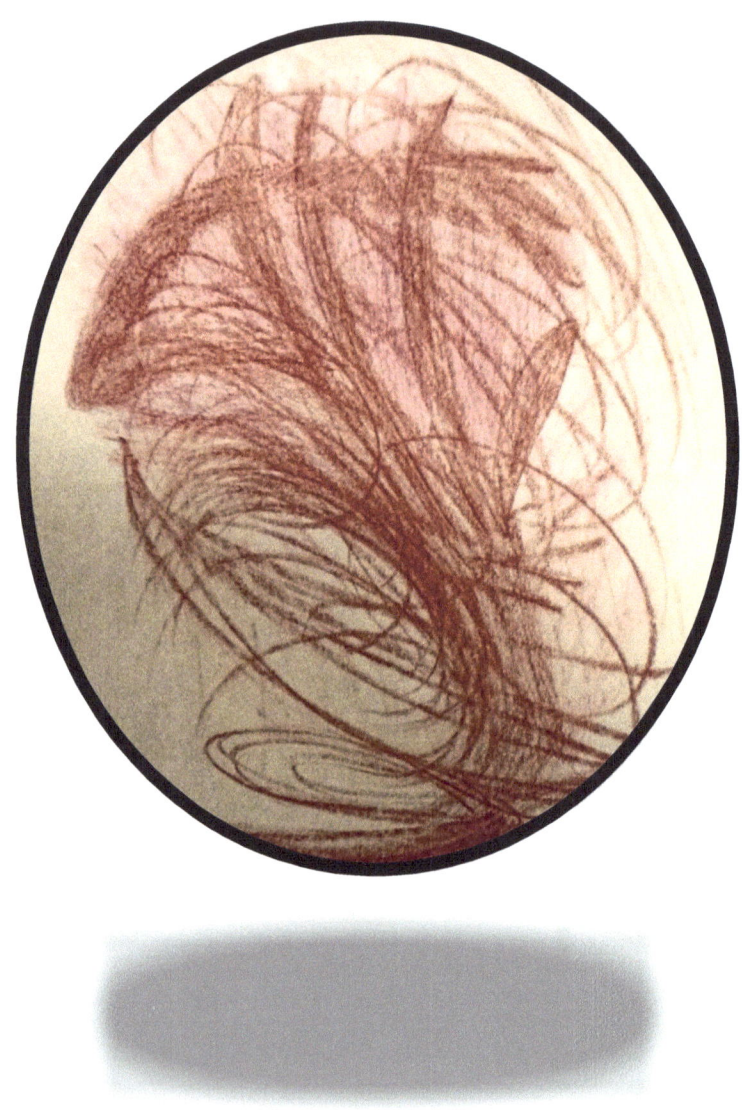

"Changing"

This book was a change for me.

"The book of scribbles"

Scribble scrabble

Will be wobble…wibble wobble

Remember the weeble

It never wobbled

Yes it did

It always wobbled

It never fell

No it never fell

Yes it did

It always fell

It never stayed down

That is right

It always got up

It always got up

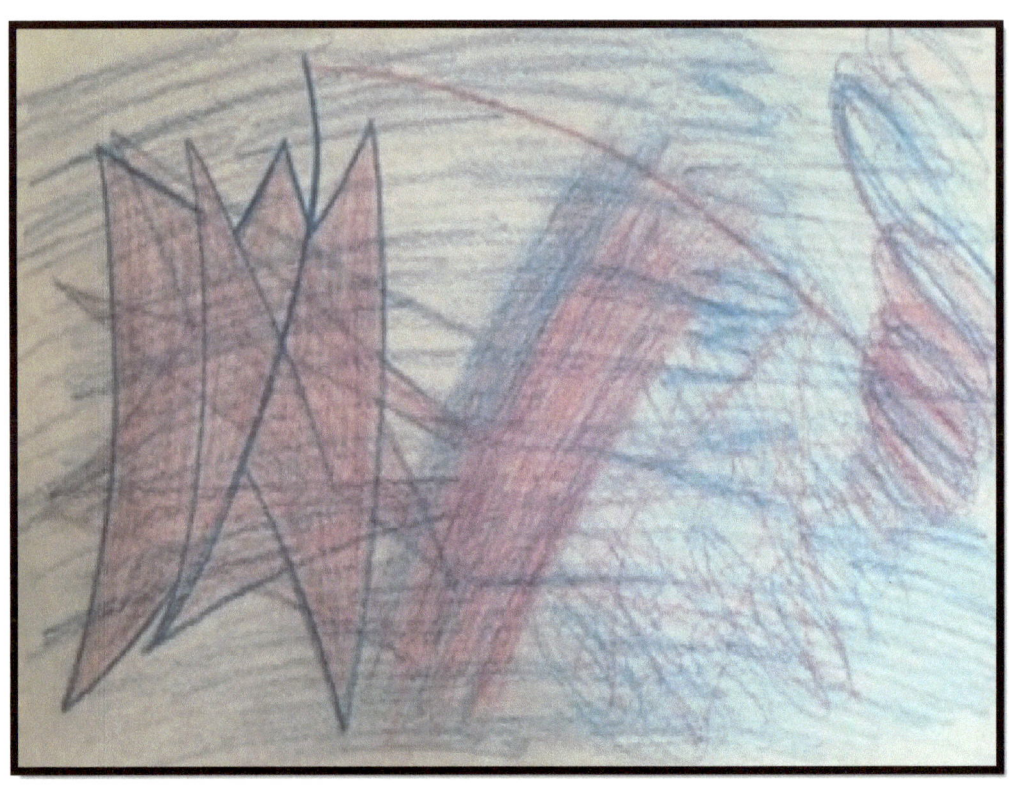

"Fishing Across the Universe"

Caught a fish!

It didn't get away!

I snared it!

Wiggling in my net!

It still has the hook

I'll take it out

I'll put it back

In the water free

It was just a game

I don't need to keep it

forever.

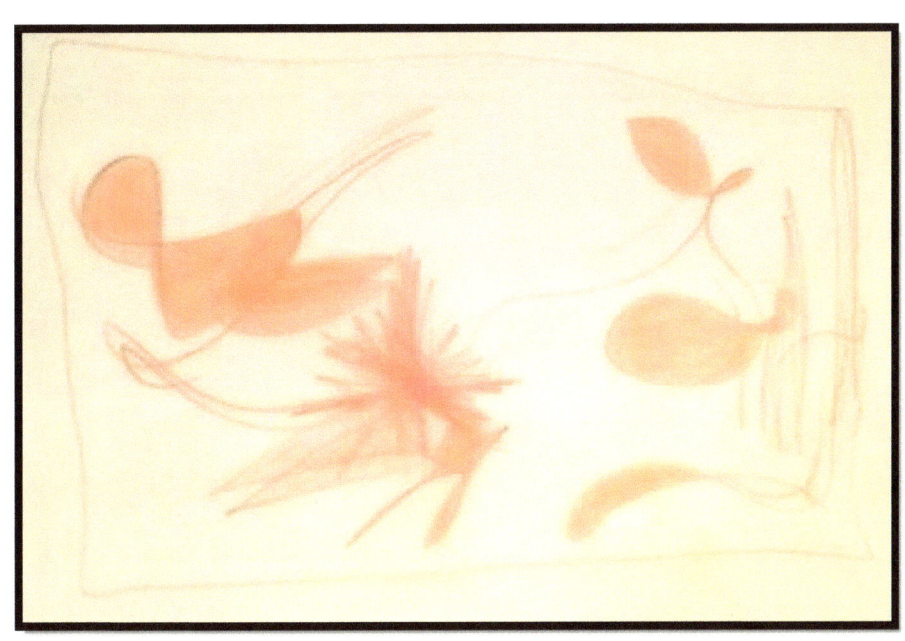

"Evolution Revolution"

Revolt of the e-volt

Volt – name after the Italian Physicist

A measure of electric potential

The potential to evolve

Evolve to revolve

Around and Around our earth went

Around and Around our species roamed

First in the water

Until plant life grew

It changed our world

Then onto the land

We emerged to revolt

Rebel!

Or does it go this way in the jar of life?

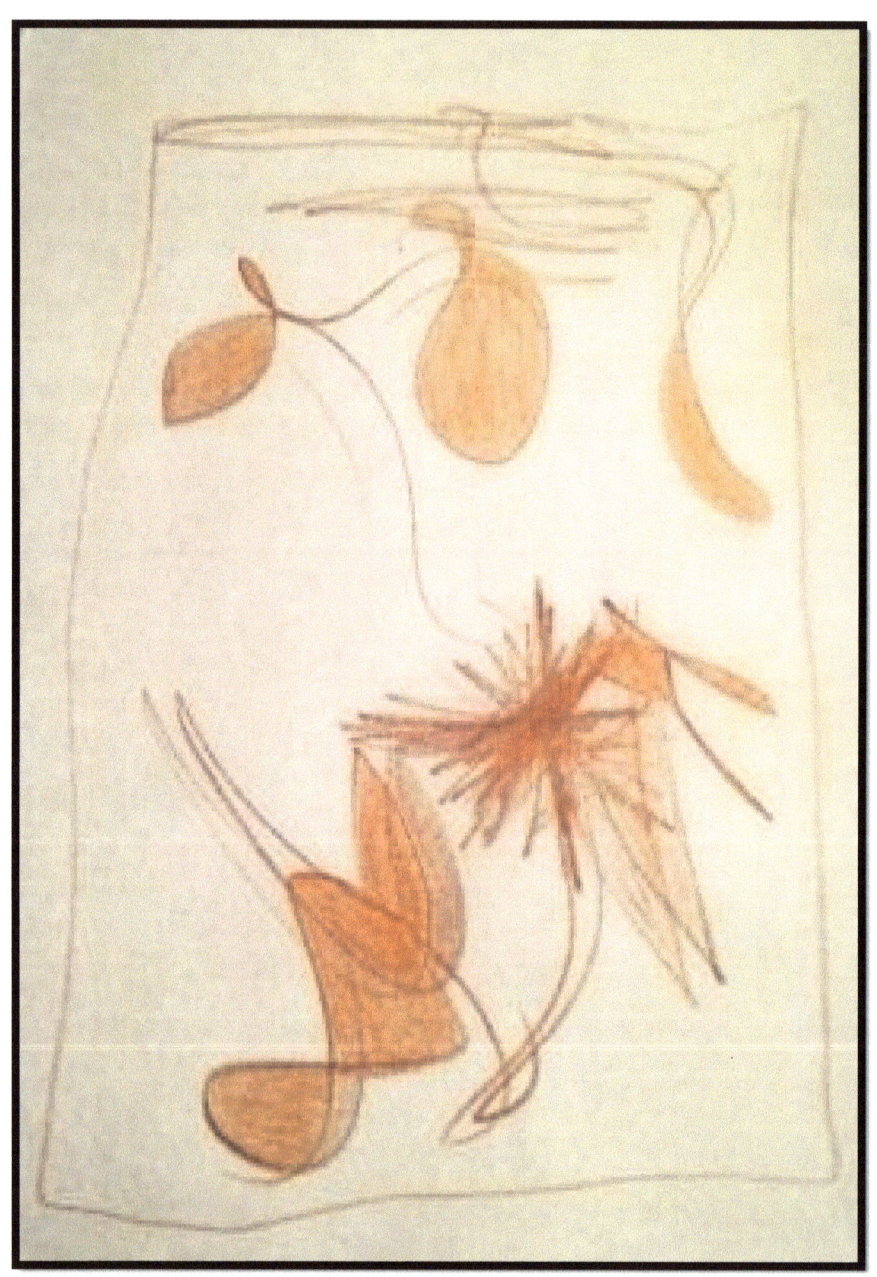

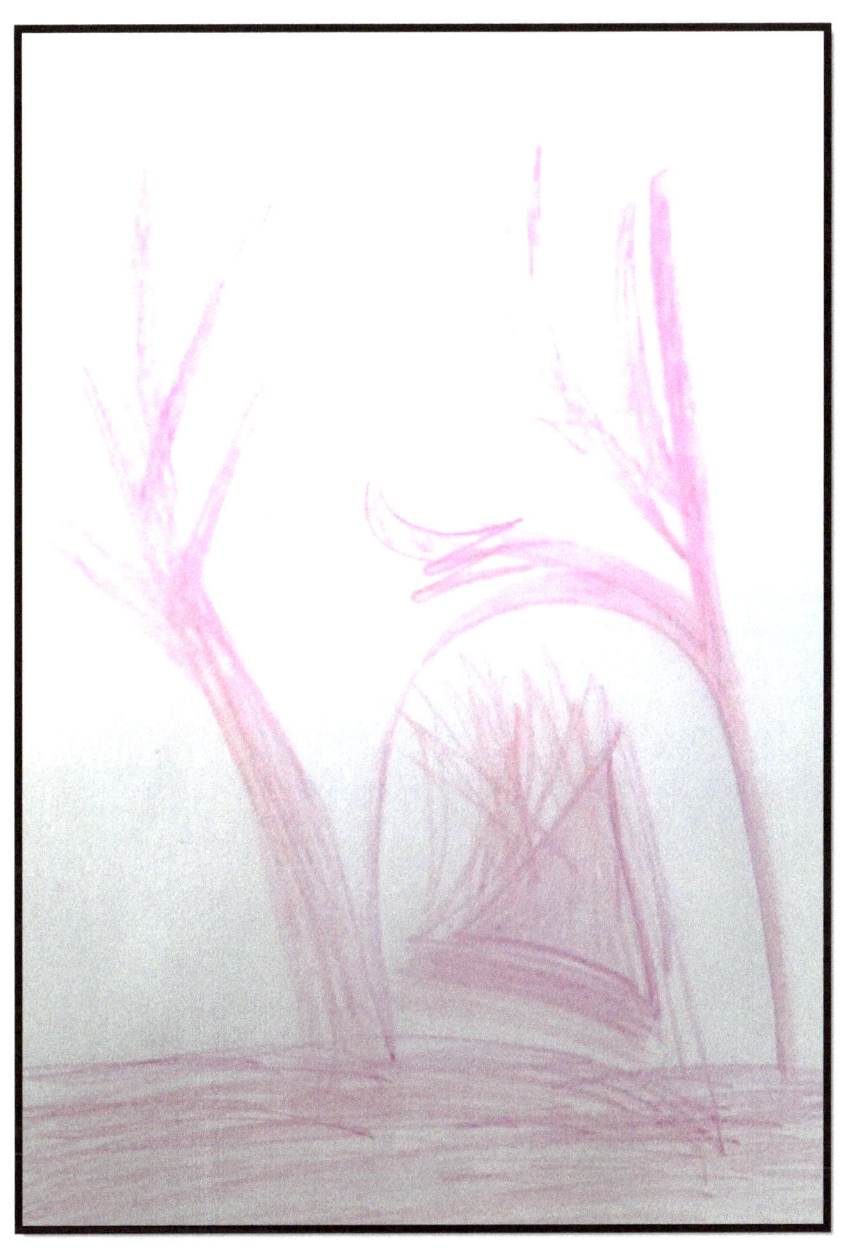

"The Other Treee"

A dead one A live 1

Why did it die?

Why can't it live

Like the other one?

Empty and barren

Not growing and flowering

It still stands there

An empty root

It'll be there for a long time

Unless someone chops it down

Or pulls it up

Dead or Alive

It'll be there for

A long Time

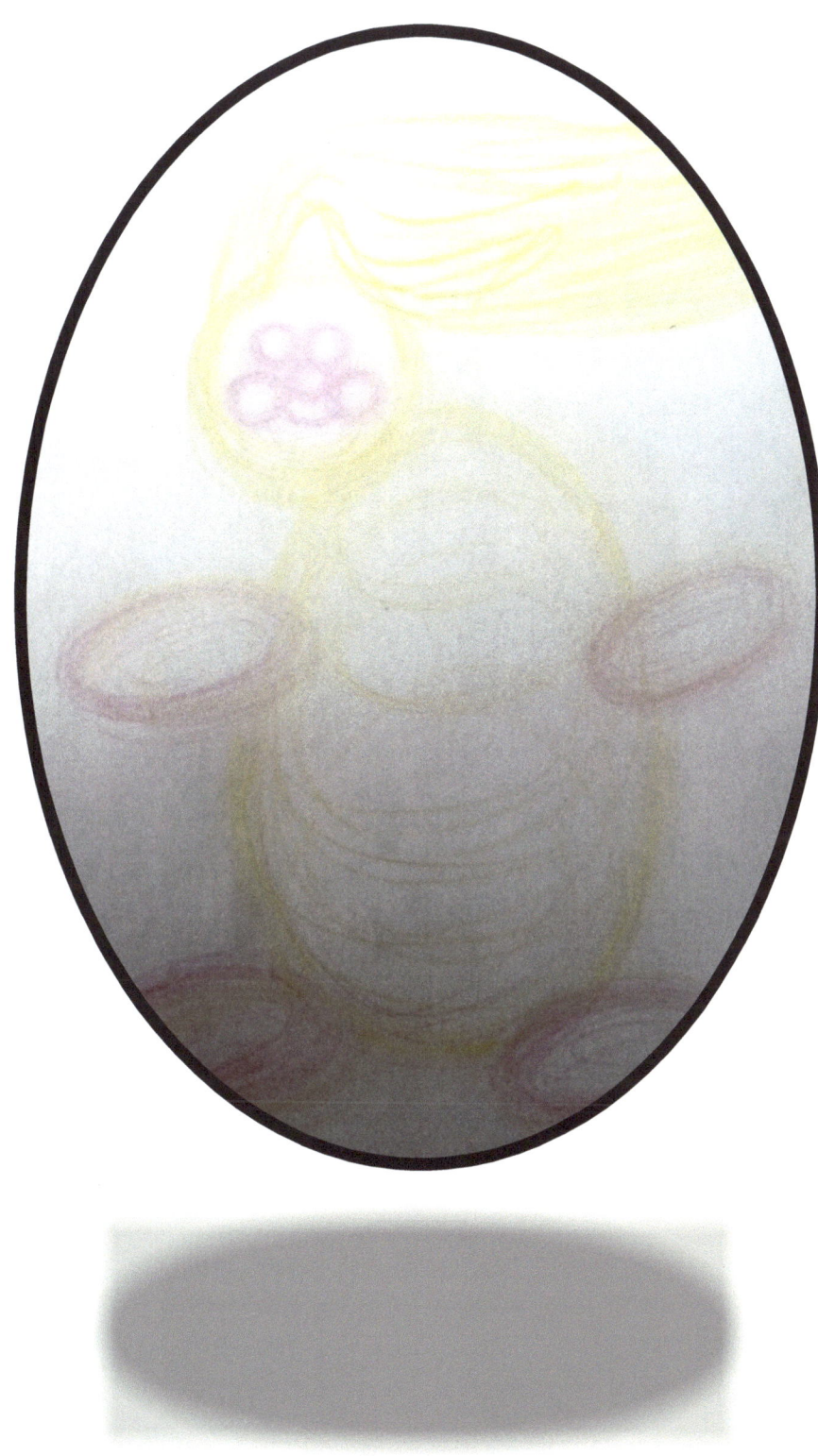

"Bunny Bug-Lady Turtle"

I loved her from the start

I was tortured by her face

I spent a lot of time on it

I thought in the end

That it should be masked

The color blurred

So you could not see her well

But in the end

I lift…left her alone

The face clear

So you could see it

Clearly

Not masked

Just plain

No mask

Not changed

Just her

"Haunted House"

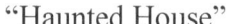

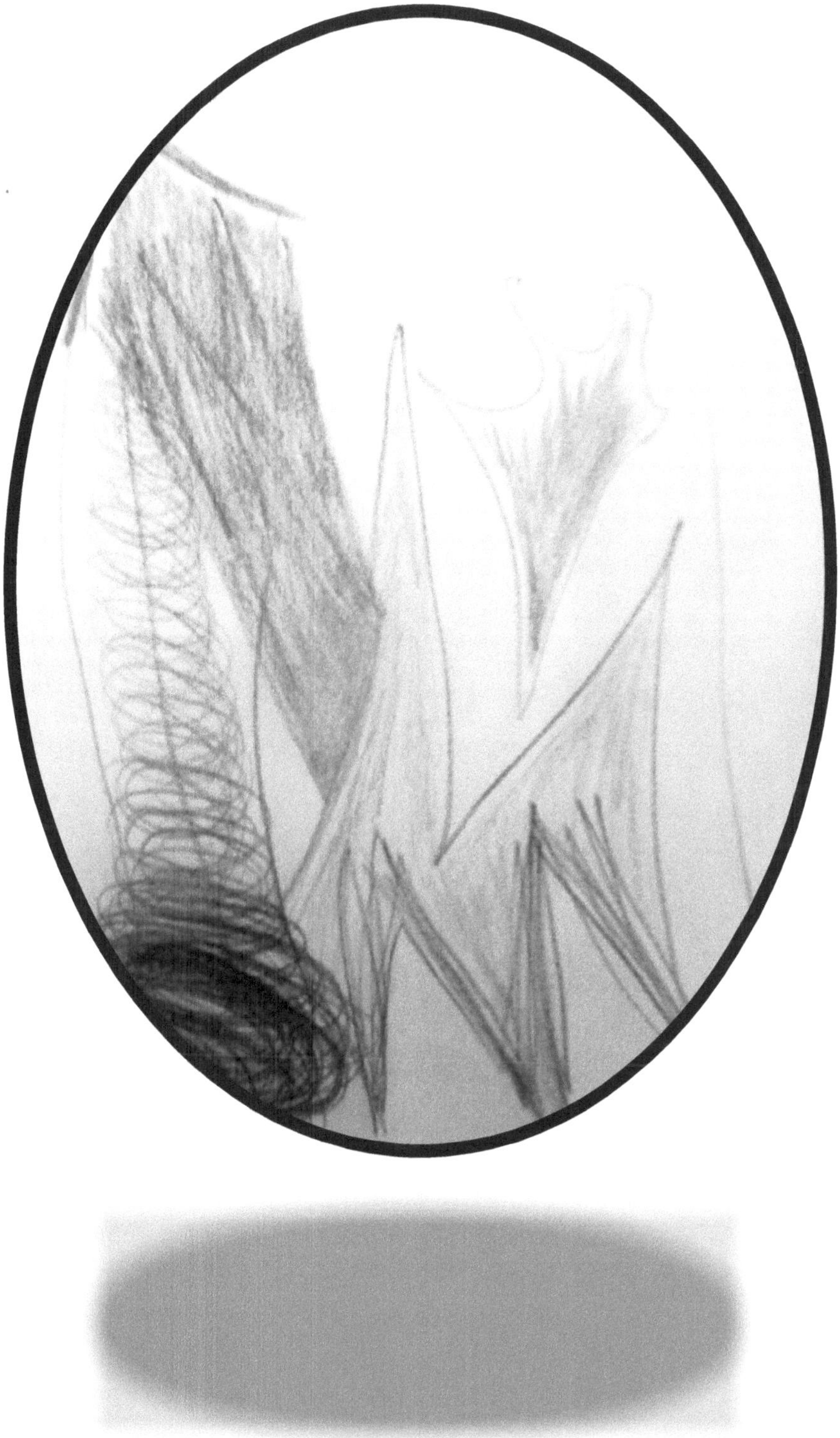

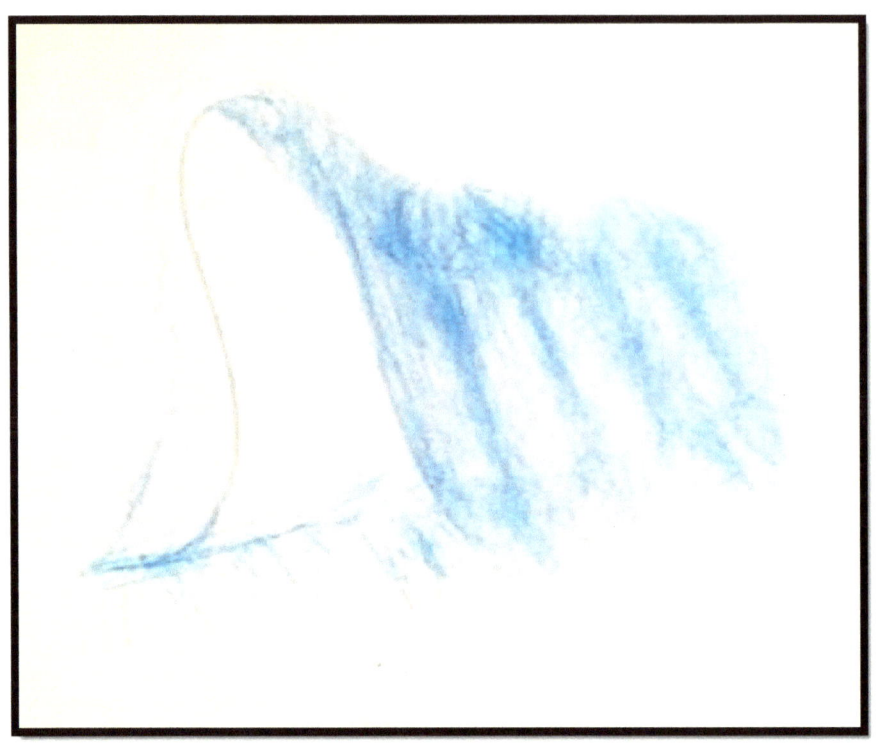

"What is this?"

I do not know yet

That is often how it is

It took me over a month to see the

"Hand of Heven" picture

I had to look at it

From across the bedroom

In the mirror

Then I saw it

The girl kneeling down

Praying

It hangs over my bed

So I can remember

To kneel

Down

And

Pray

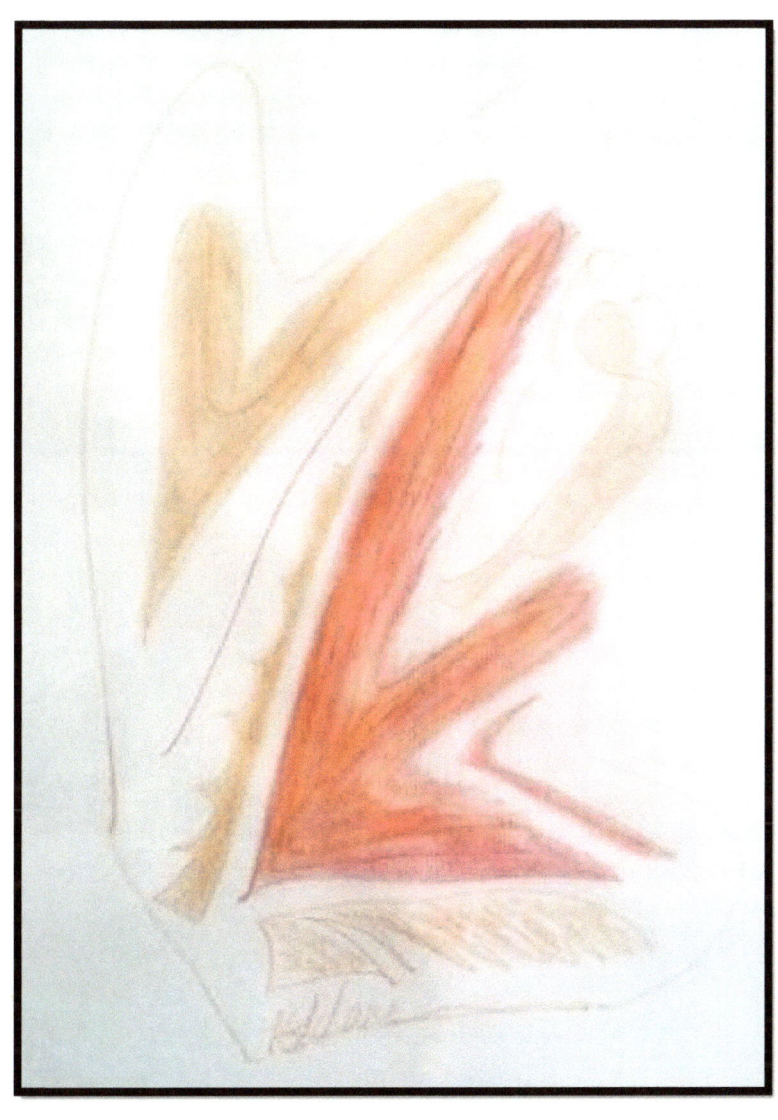

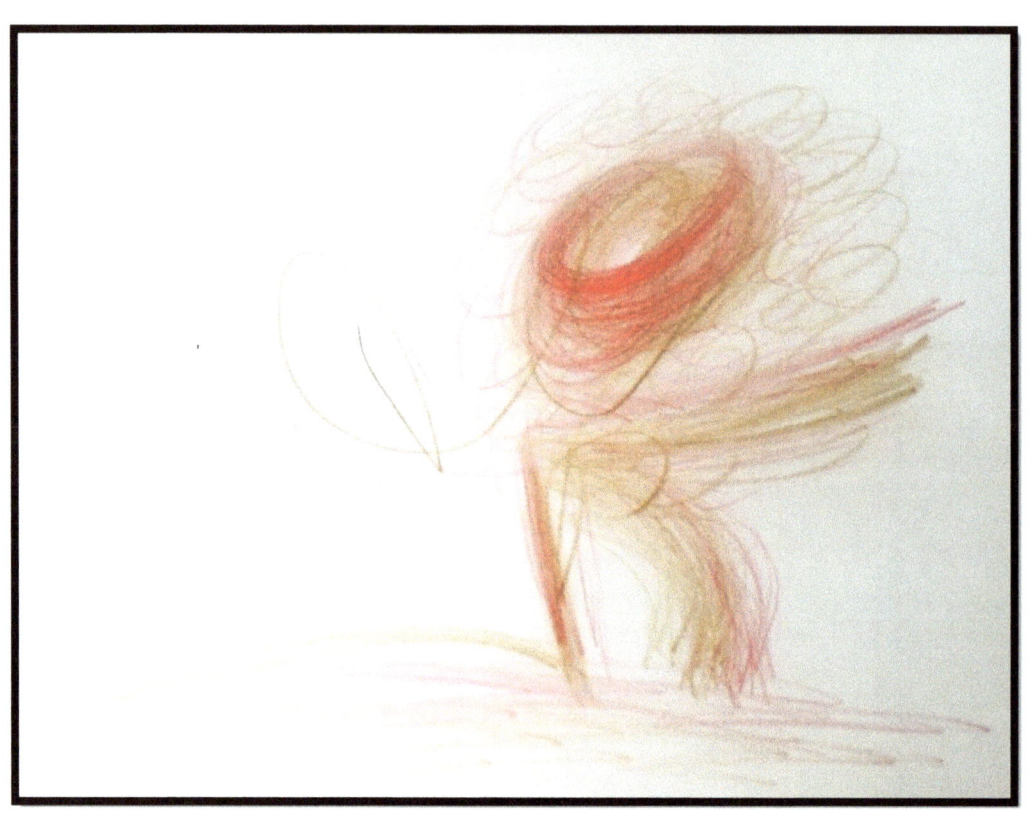

"A Flower or An Angel"

They said right away

They could see An Angel

I still see

A Flower

Different people will see

Different Things

Or are they

actually

the same

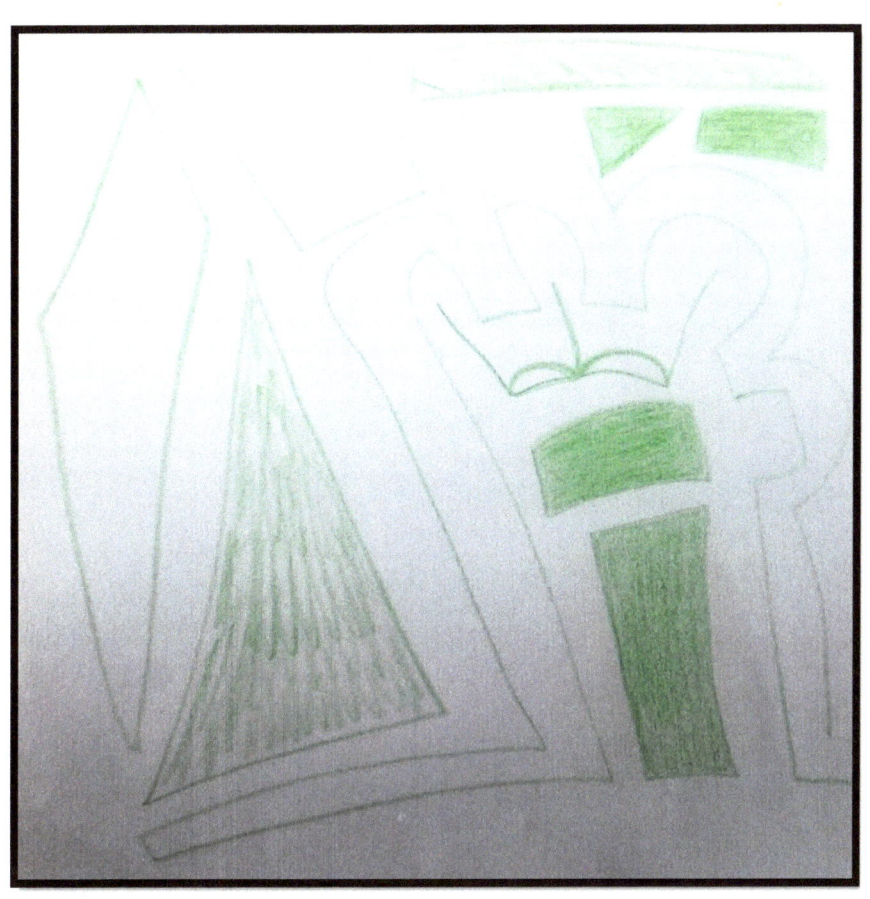

"Acastleatreeadoorawindow"

It is funny to me

How quickly

My brain

Changes tunes

From one drawing

To the next

I drew a lot of these one

Right after the other

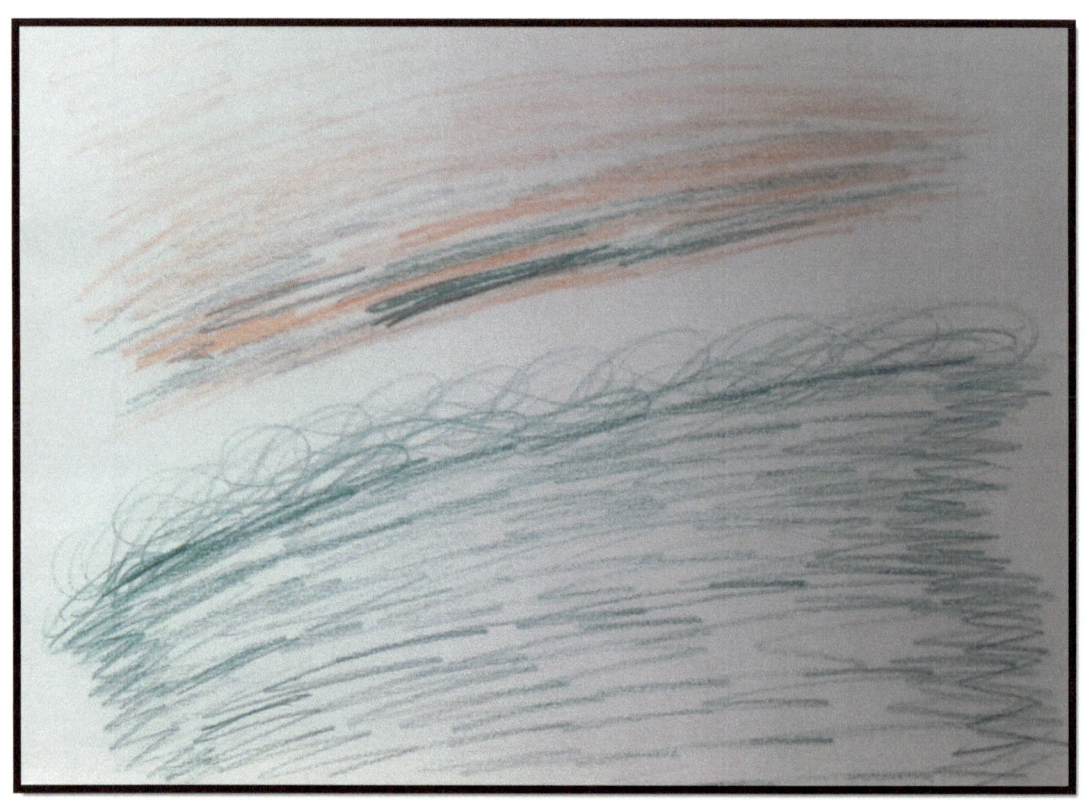

"Sun ride…rise or set"

Whether

It is up or down

It is true

It will take you on a ride

Up or down

The ride

As you wonder

How

Could it be

So beautiful

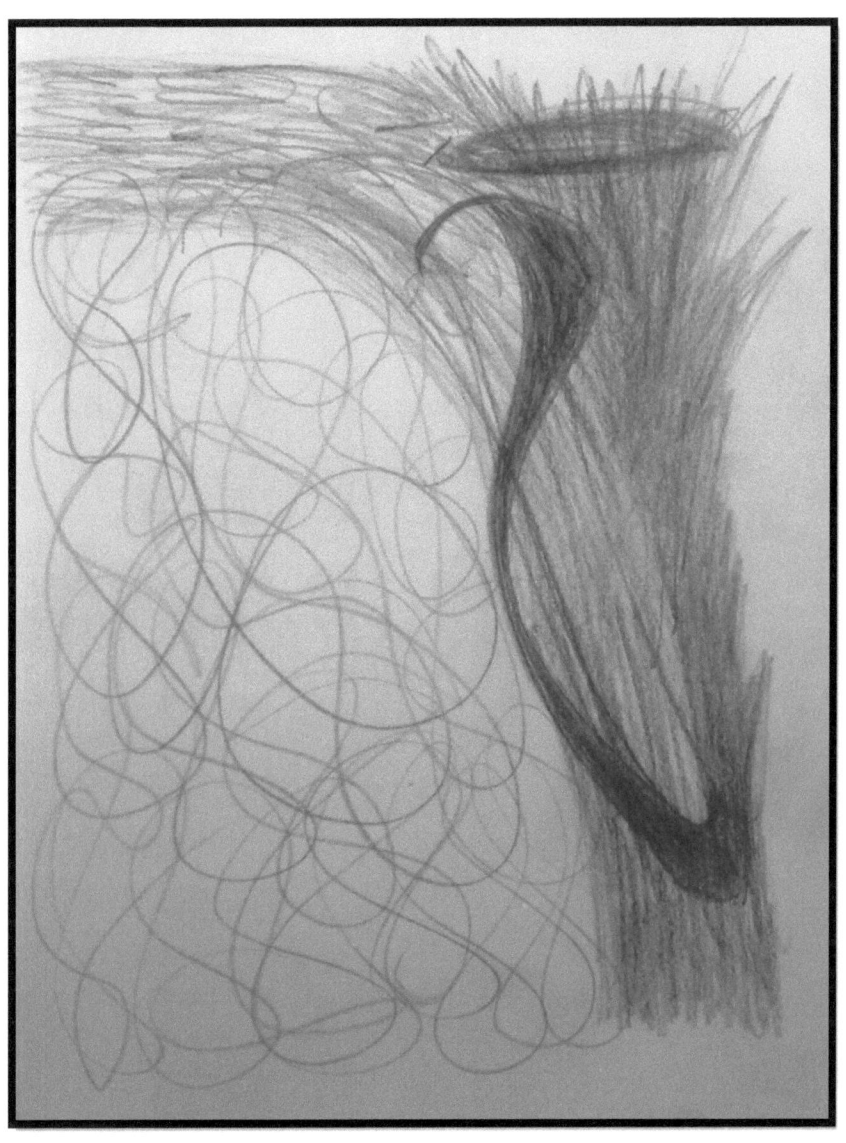

"The serpent's soul"

He does have one

A soul

He does have one

A snake

Or is it a puppy dog's tail

Even the devil

Had one

A sole

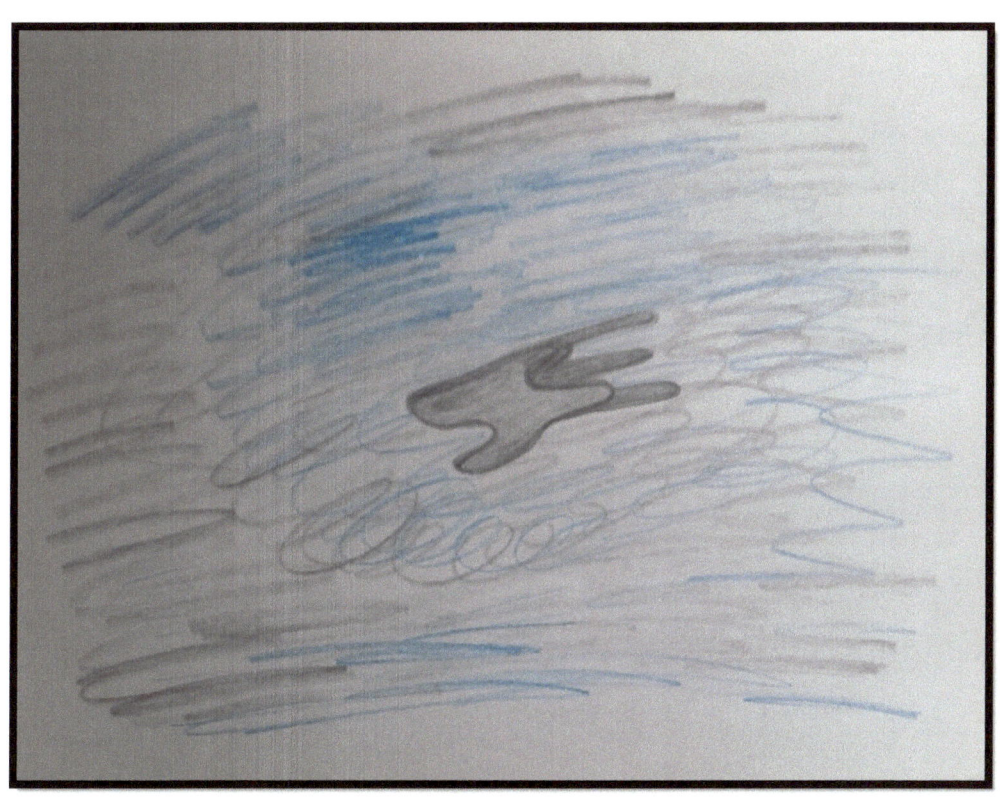

"Cloud Shapes"

The clouds move

So do the shapes

They change

From a running rabbit

To a…

"A flower Card"

Send a carp…card

Do not send a fish

In the mail

The male man

Will not like it

He does not want

His little car

To smell like fish

Send a card

With a flower

Or with anything on it

Send a card

For the birthdays and anniversaries

For the un-birthdays

And the other days

Not every day

Just the special days

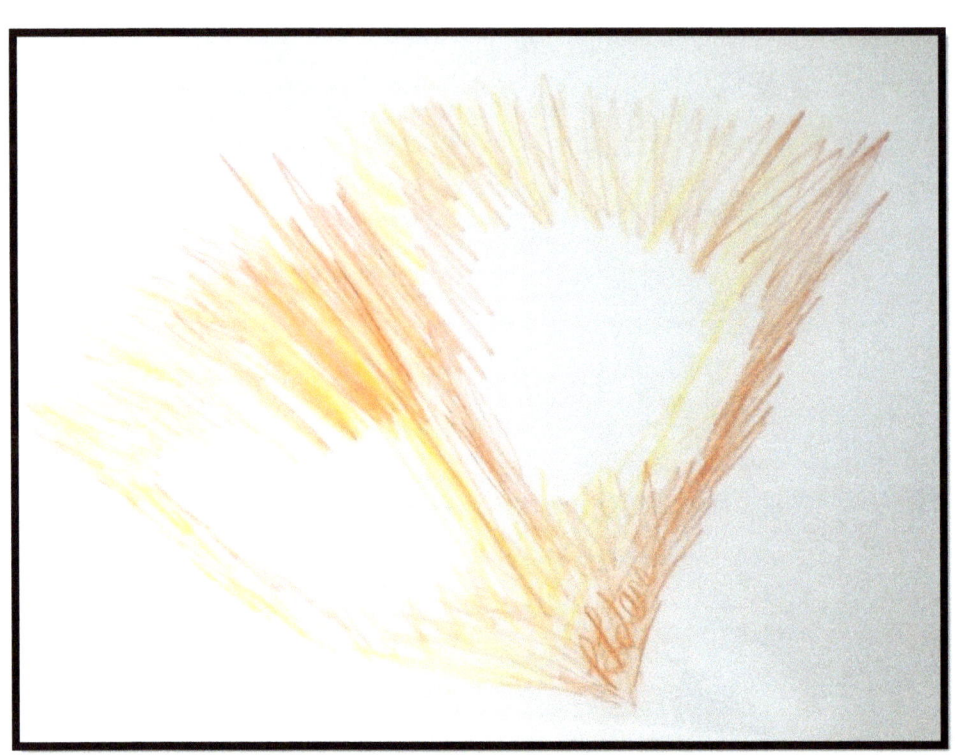

"Hard Heart"

I knew within seconds

That I was drawing a heart

Why it is…is it all scratchy like that

The edges not smooth

What does it mean?

My heart needs a smooth love

Easy and flowing

Not jagged and rough

Don't they know?

I like easy and happy

Love flow my way

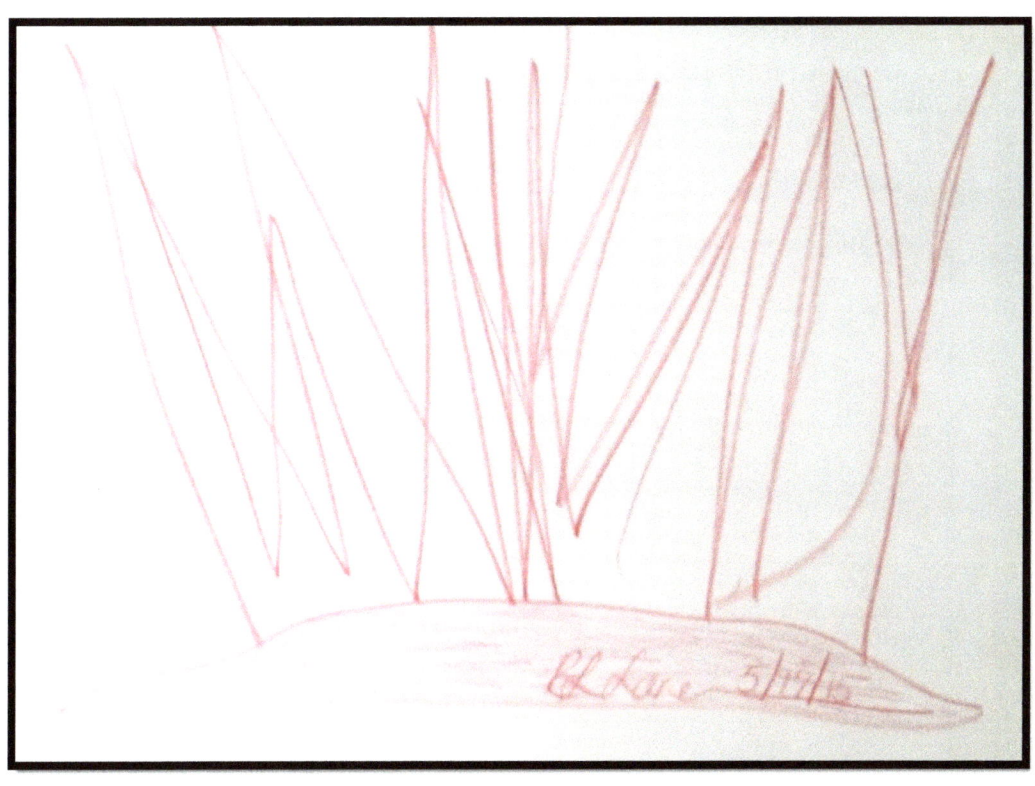

"Wendy"

Do you see it?

My name

My first name

Not my last

My only name

My first and last

First Name

I finally understood why "The Book…Bag of Scribbles" needed to be written. It was so you will better understand the illustrations within my books. The EcarreT series.

Bookbag. Did I draw a bookbag? I still don't know what this one is…

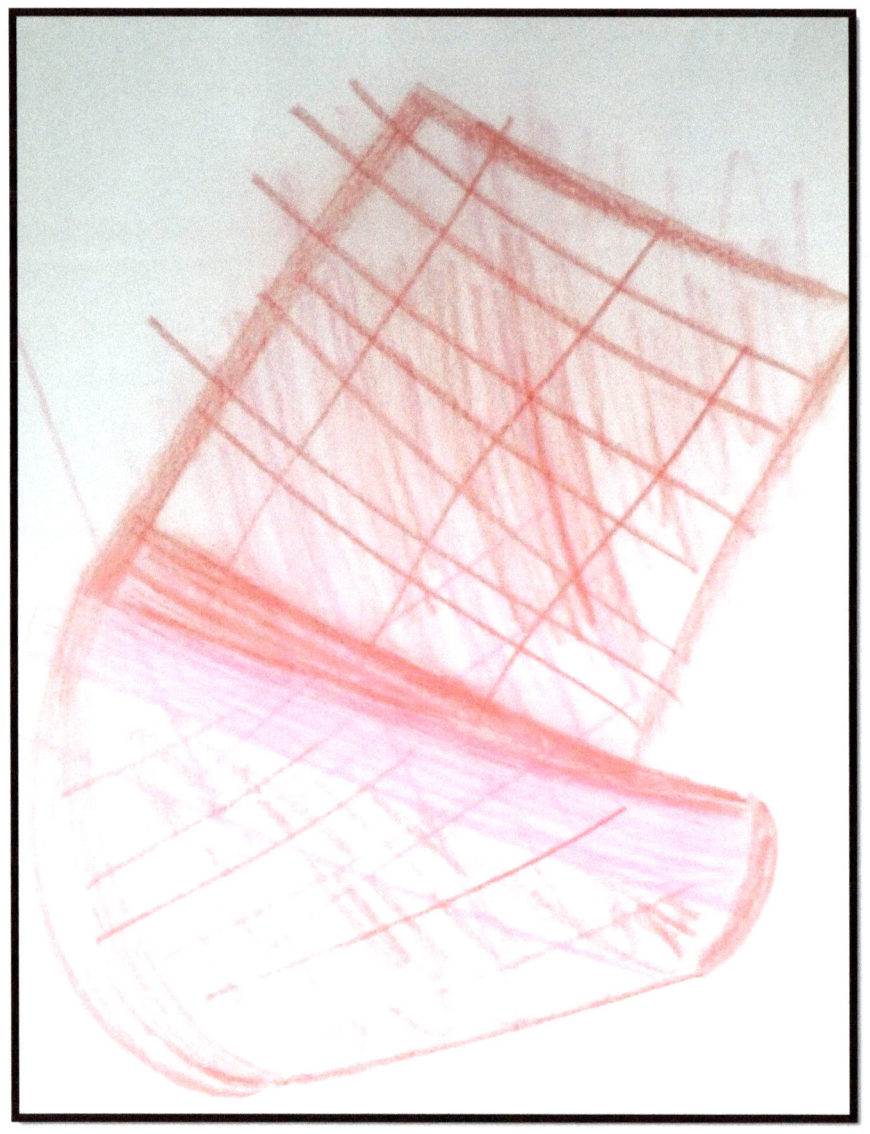

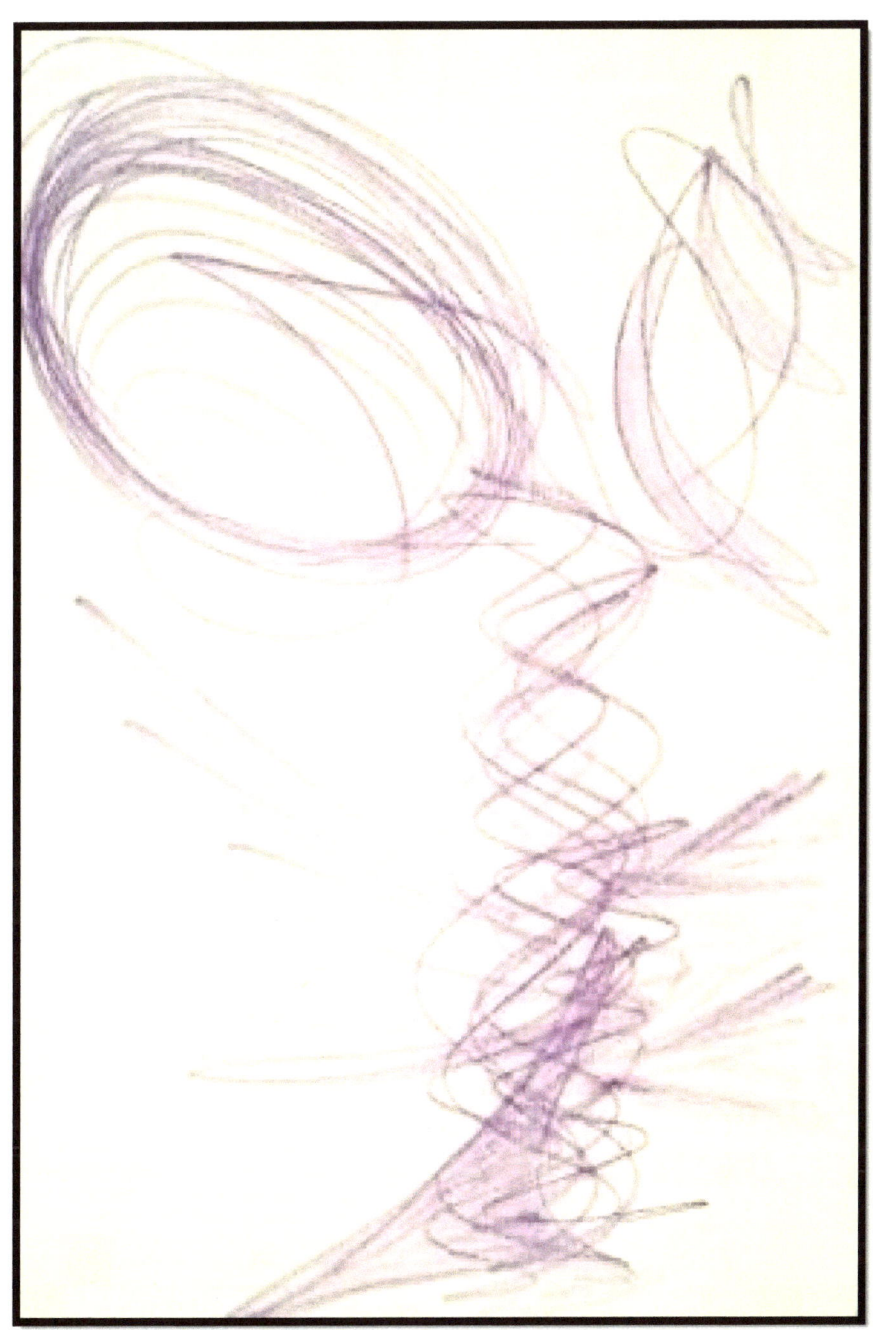

"DNA"

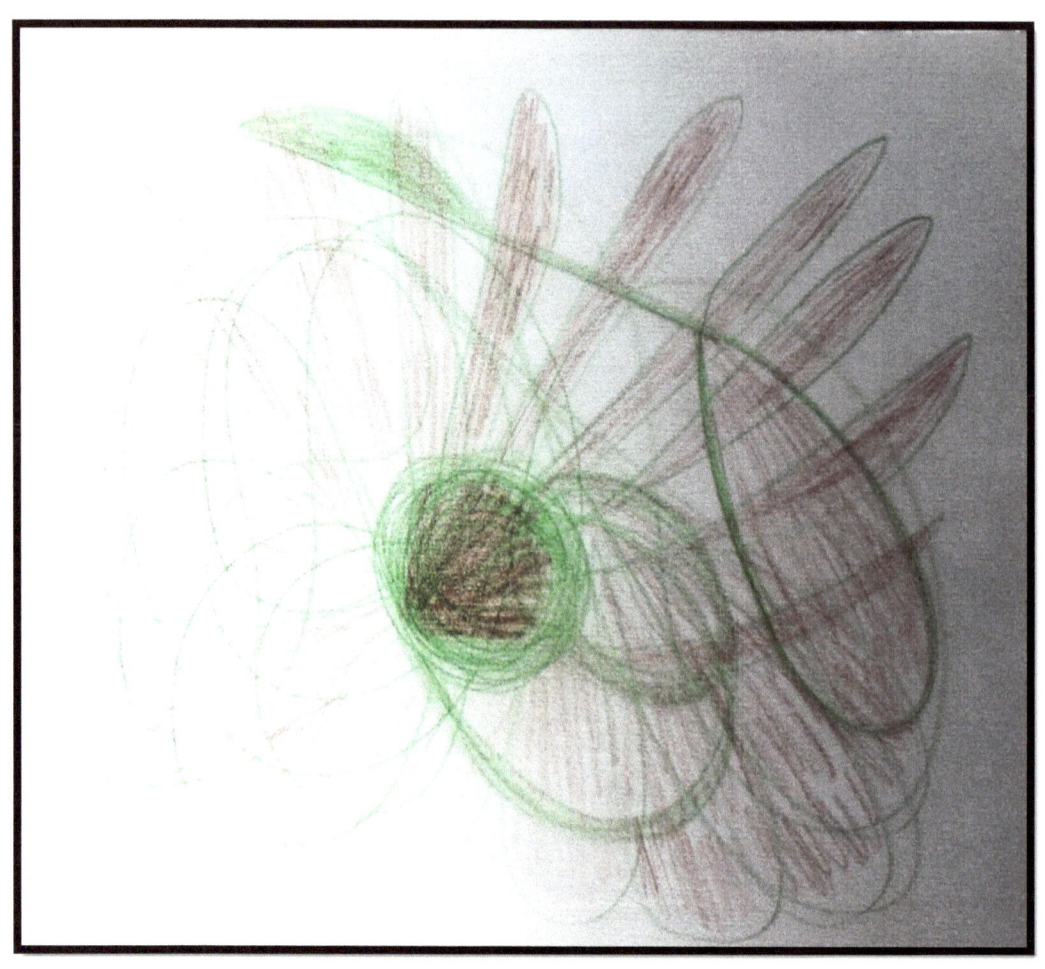

"Flower Songs"

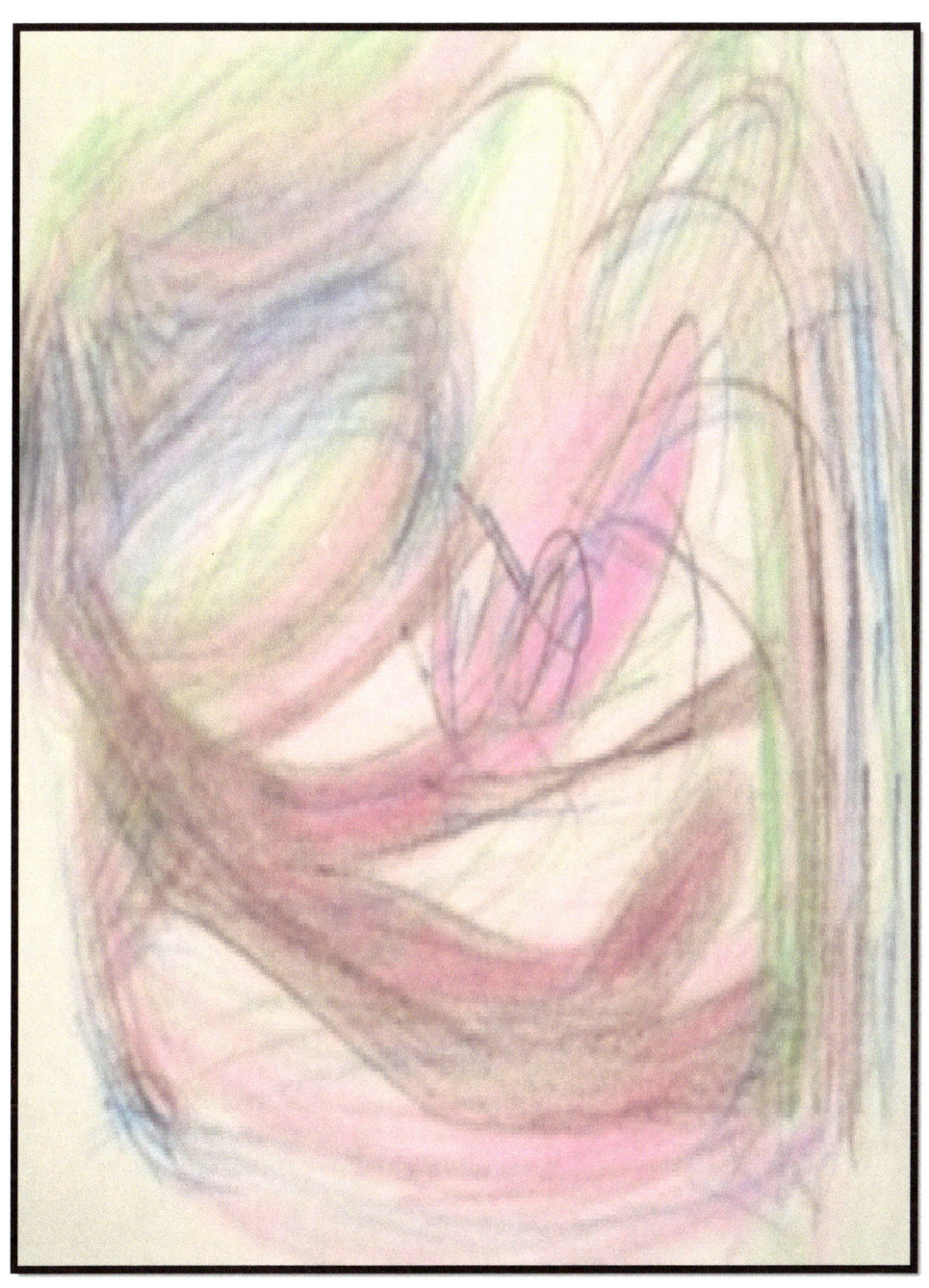

"Inside the Rainbow"

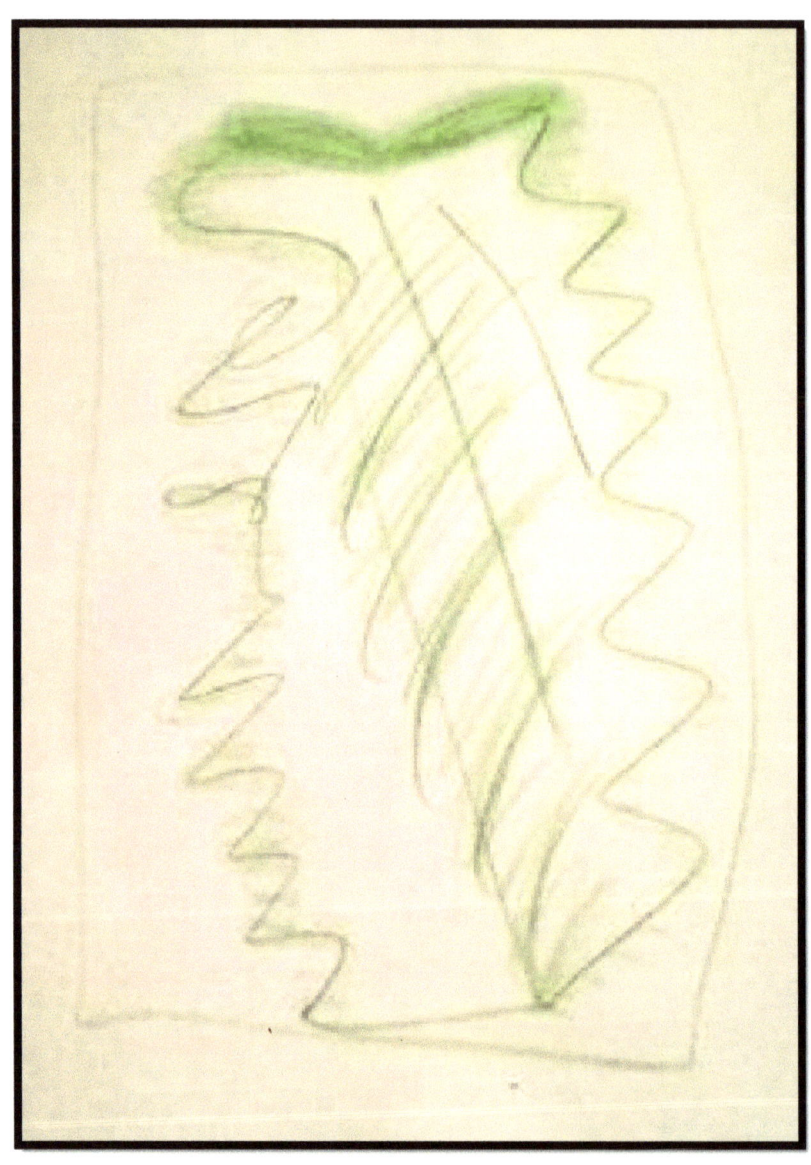

"Lady Gator"

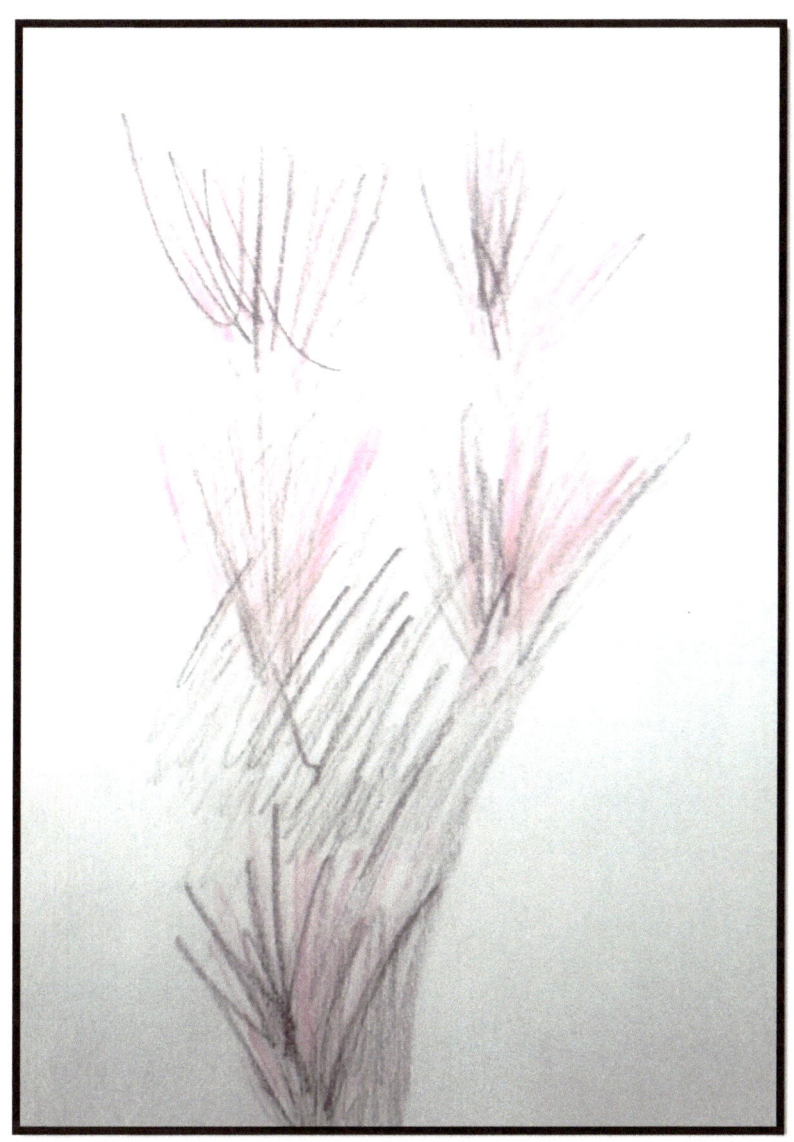

"Lillies"

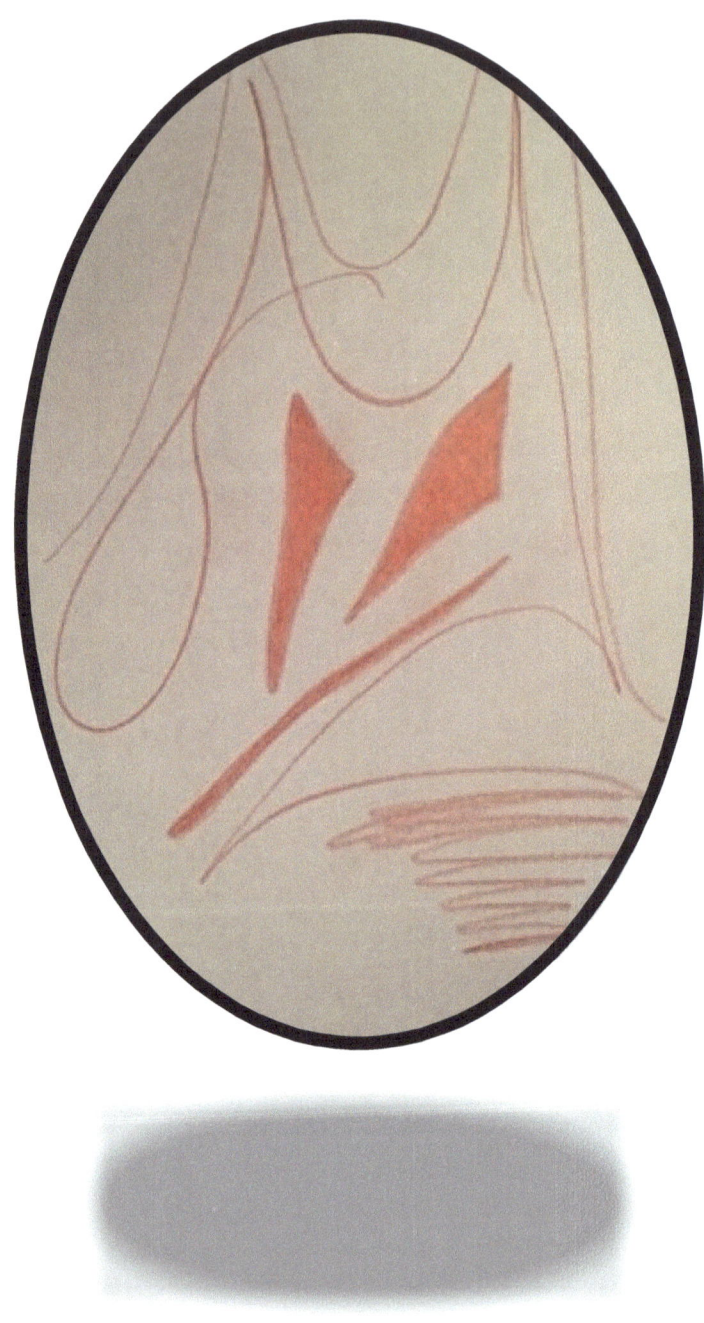

"The Mask"

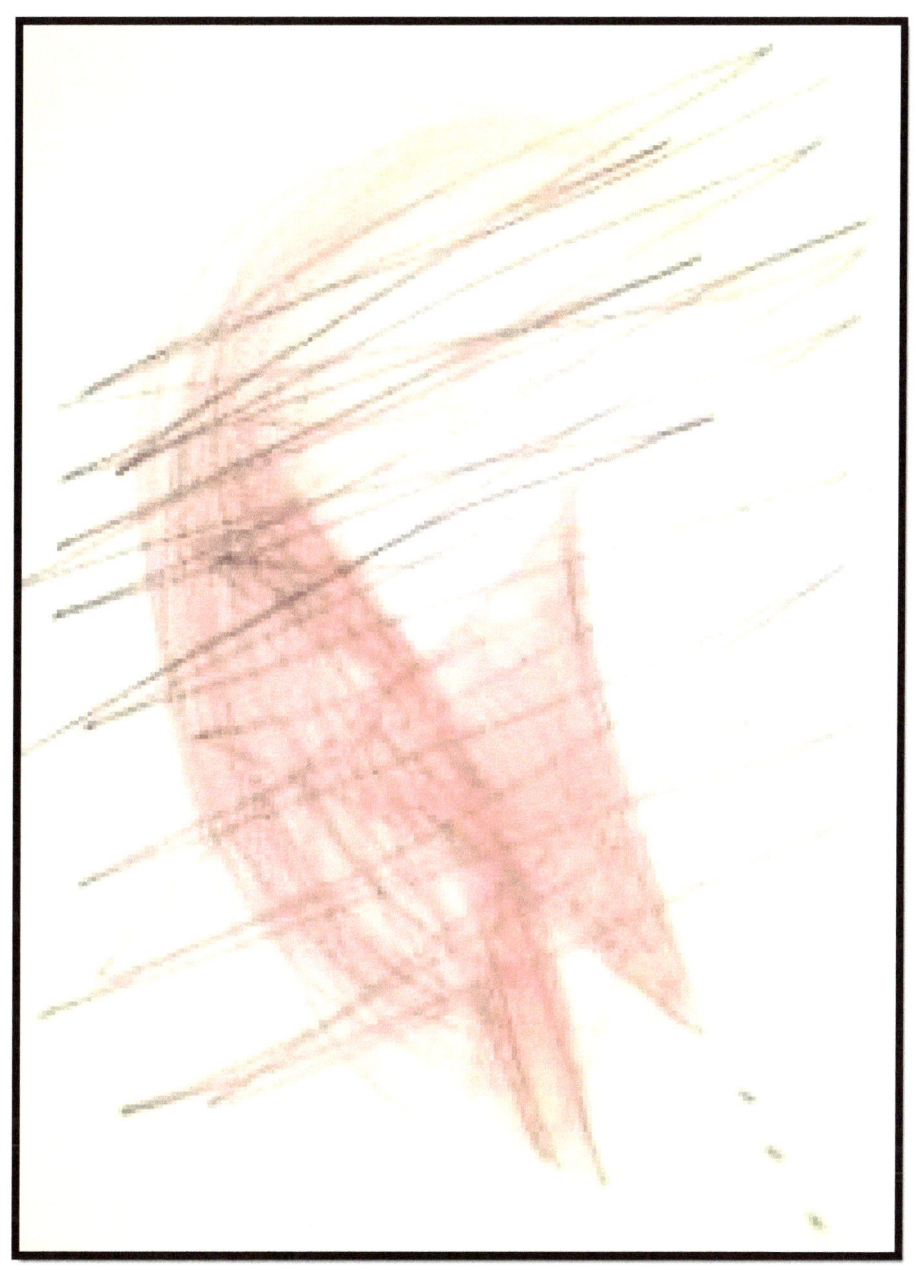

"Penguin or is that Dolphin"

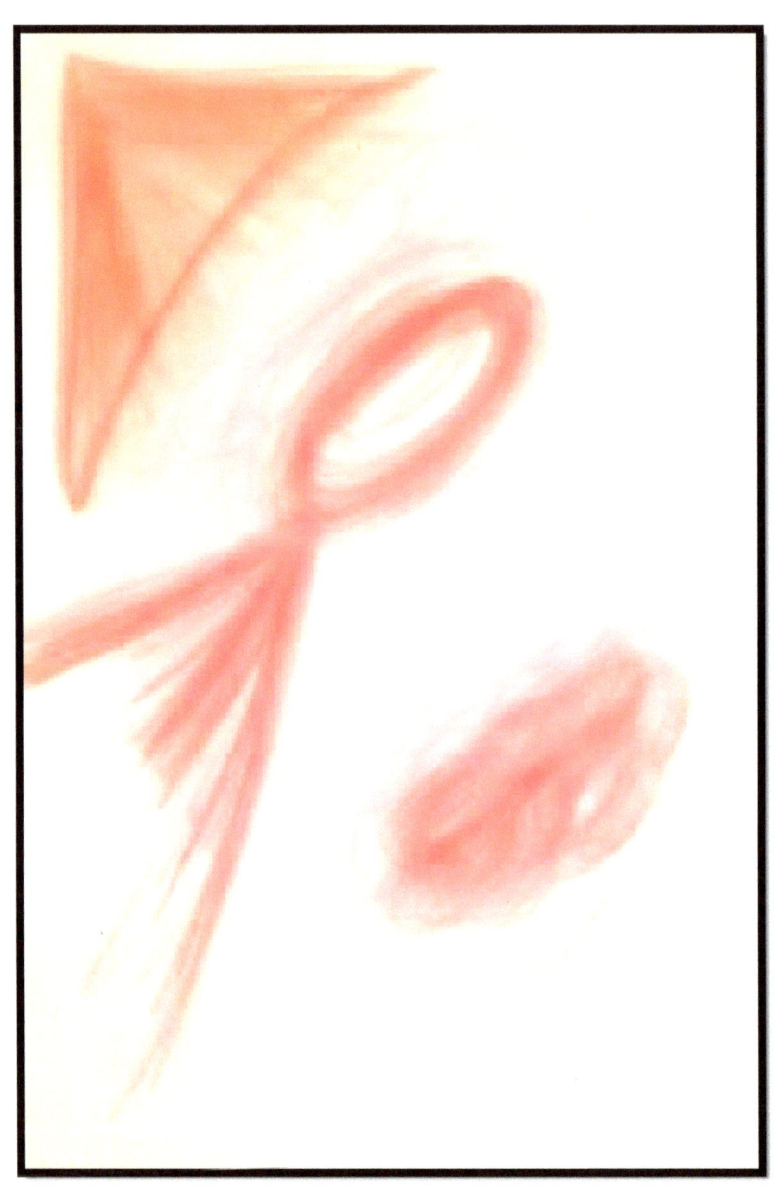

"Red Lost her Hood"

Who took it?

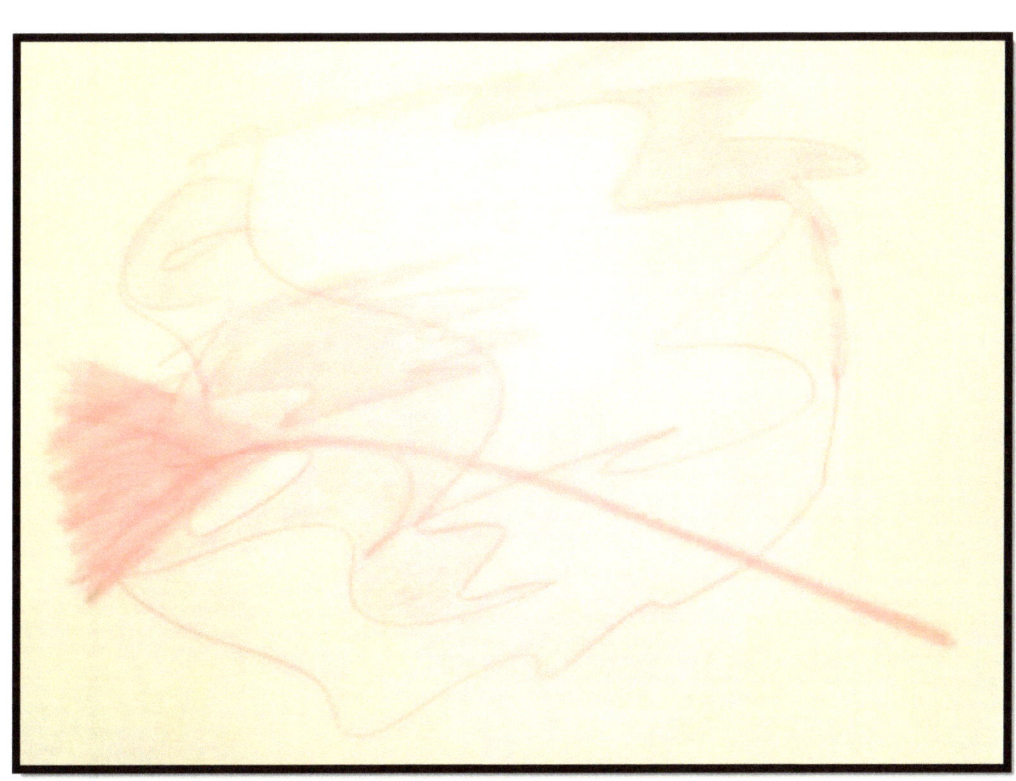

"Riding the Broom"

Who made her mad?

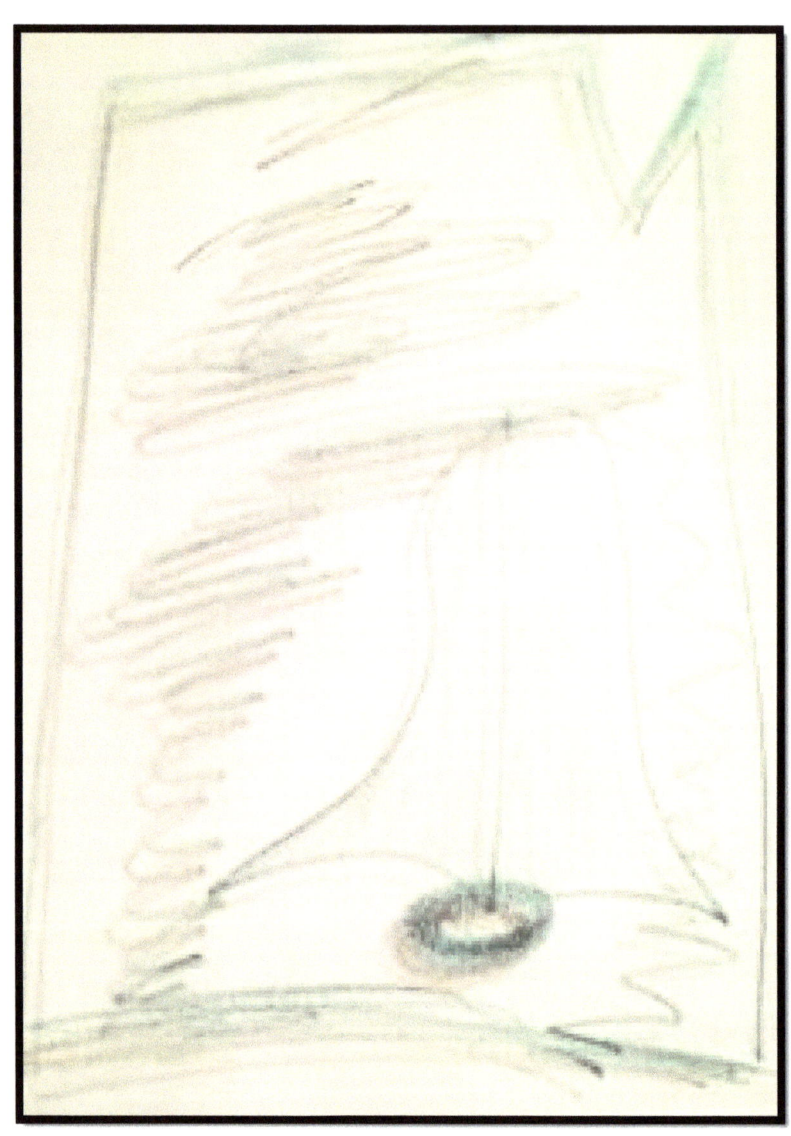

"Ringing Bell"

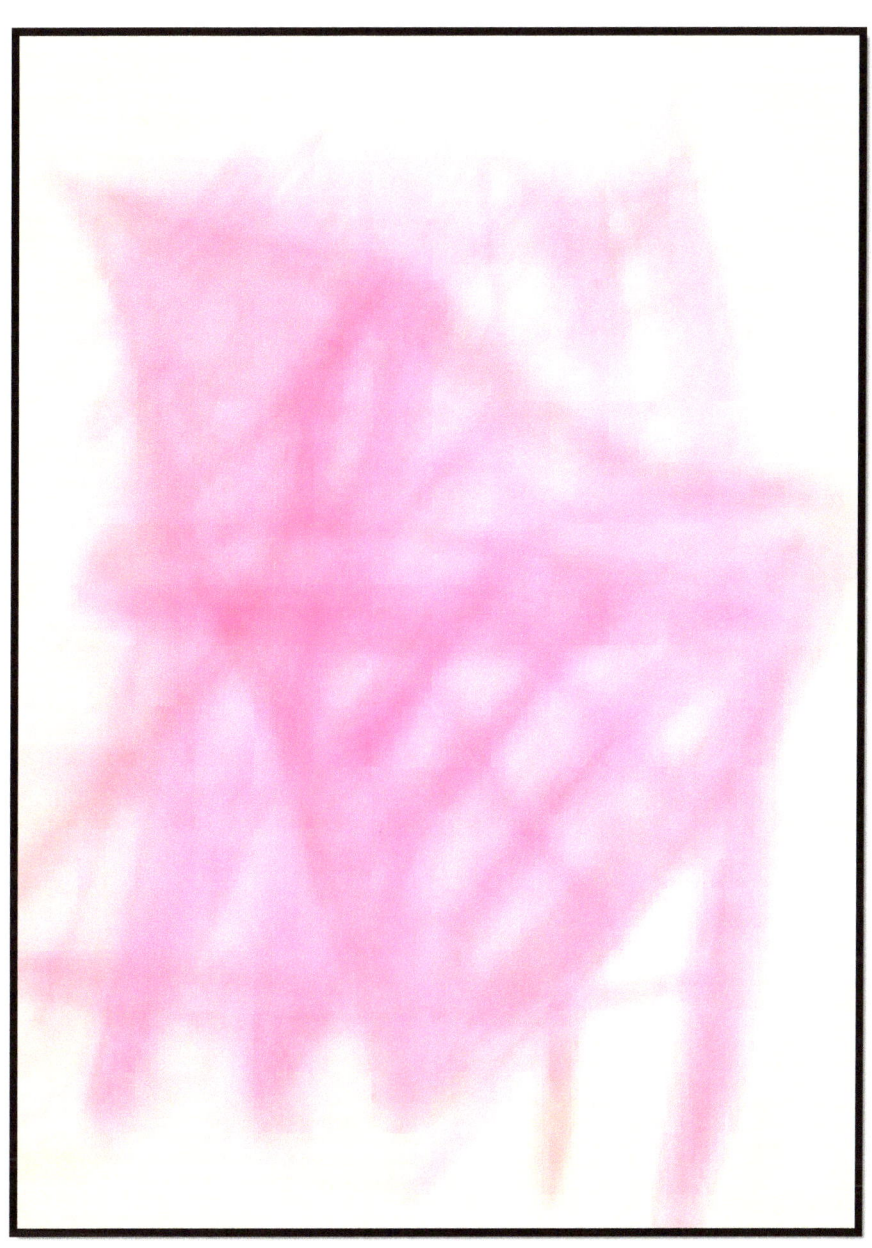

"Ringing the Bell"

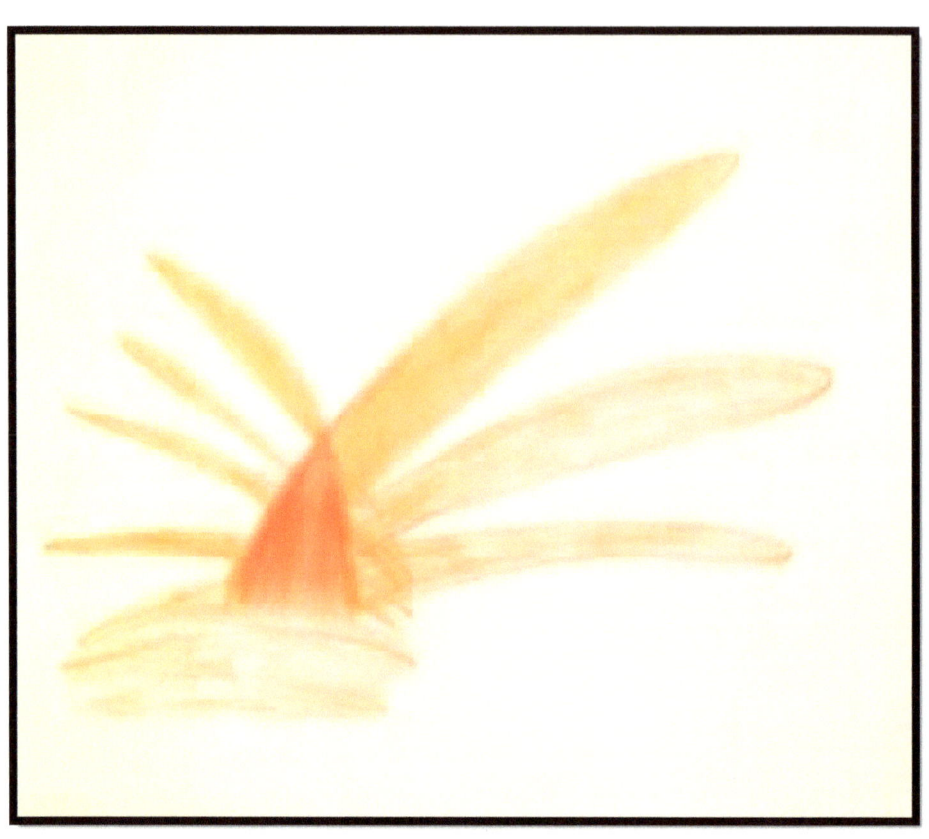

"Rocket"

This one is important…I don't know why…

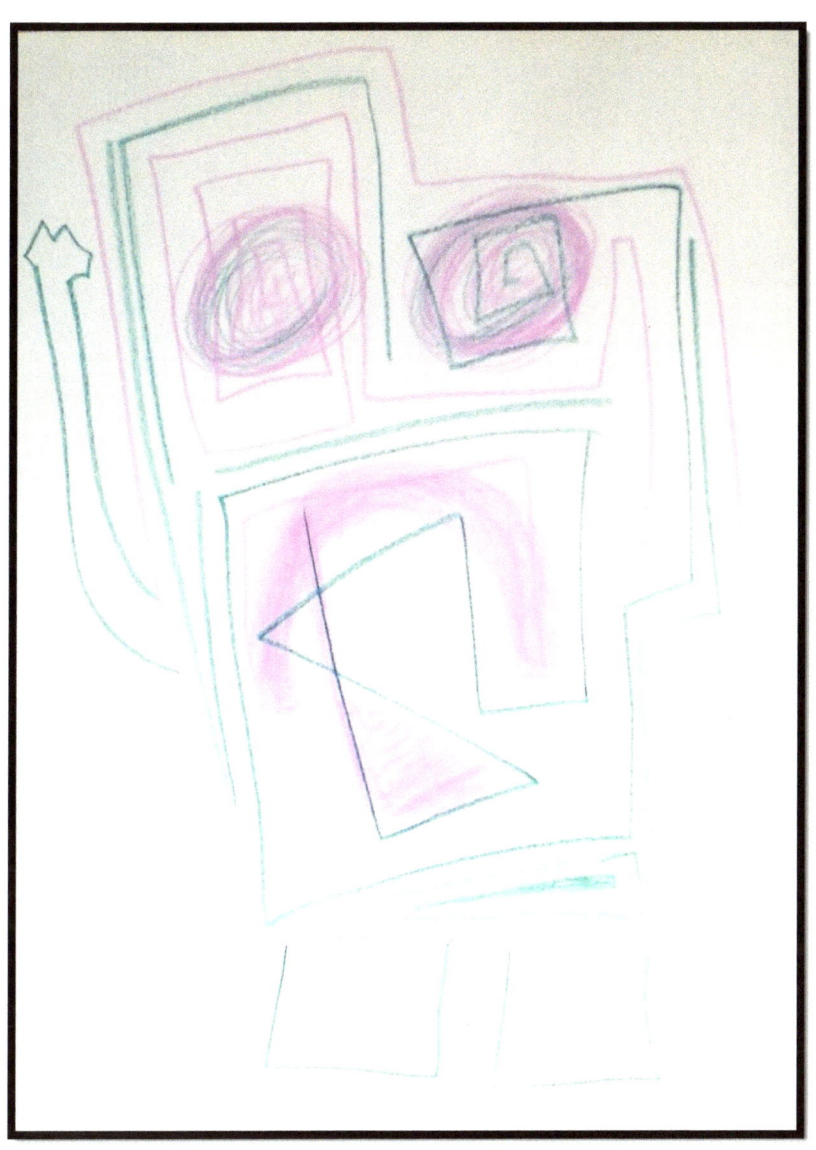

"Sal the Sad Robot"

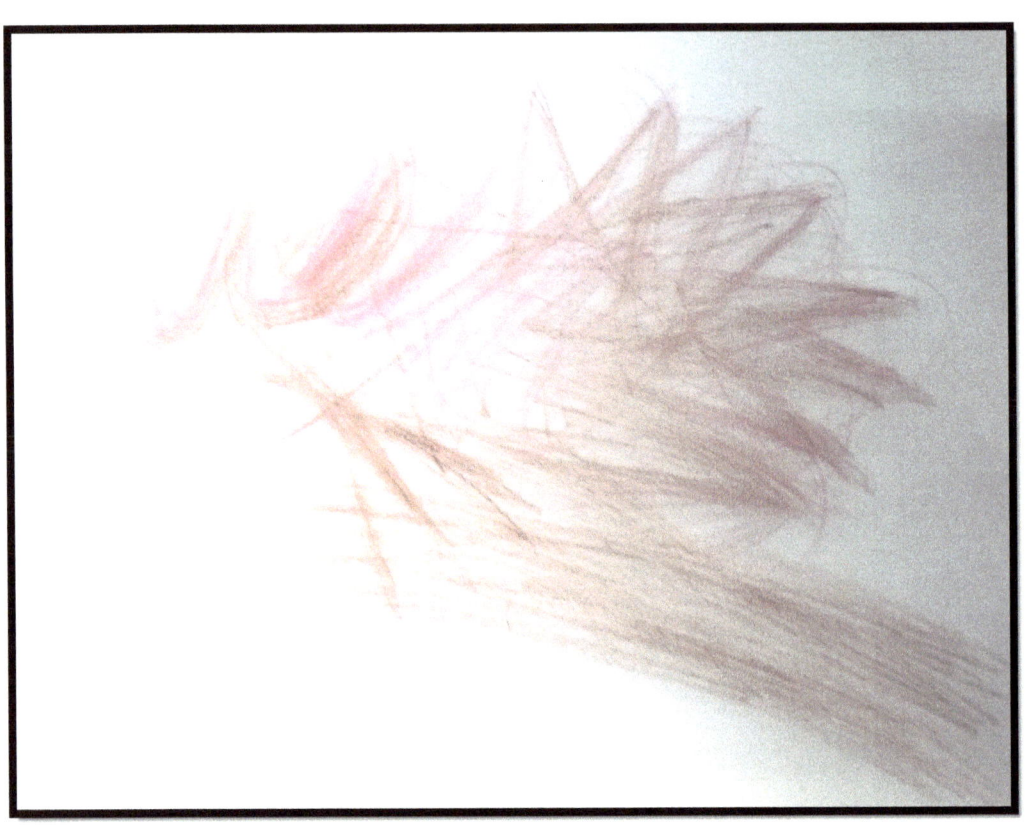

"Shooting Stars"

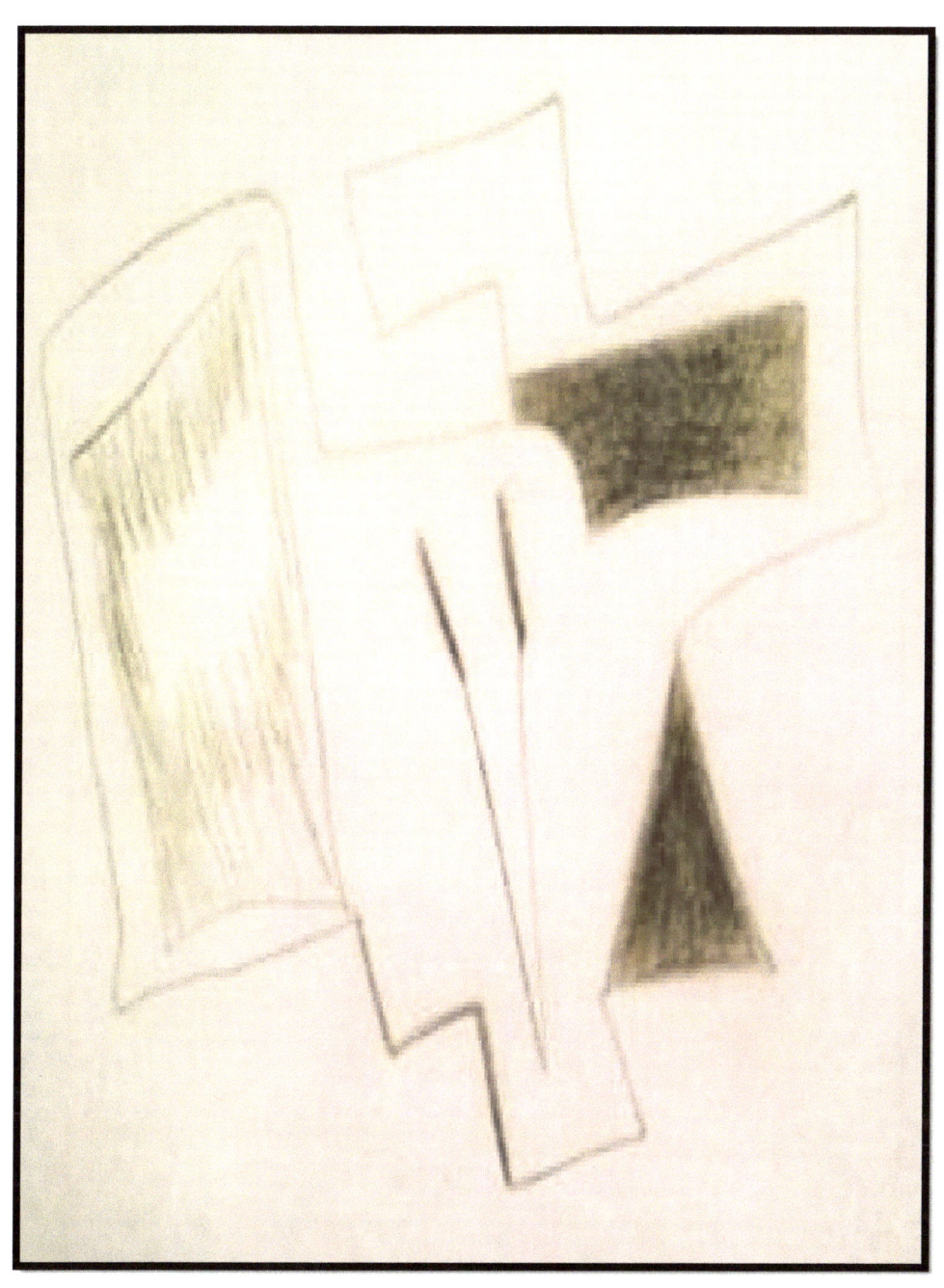

"Swamp Monster"

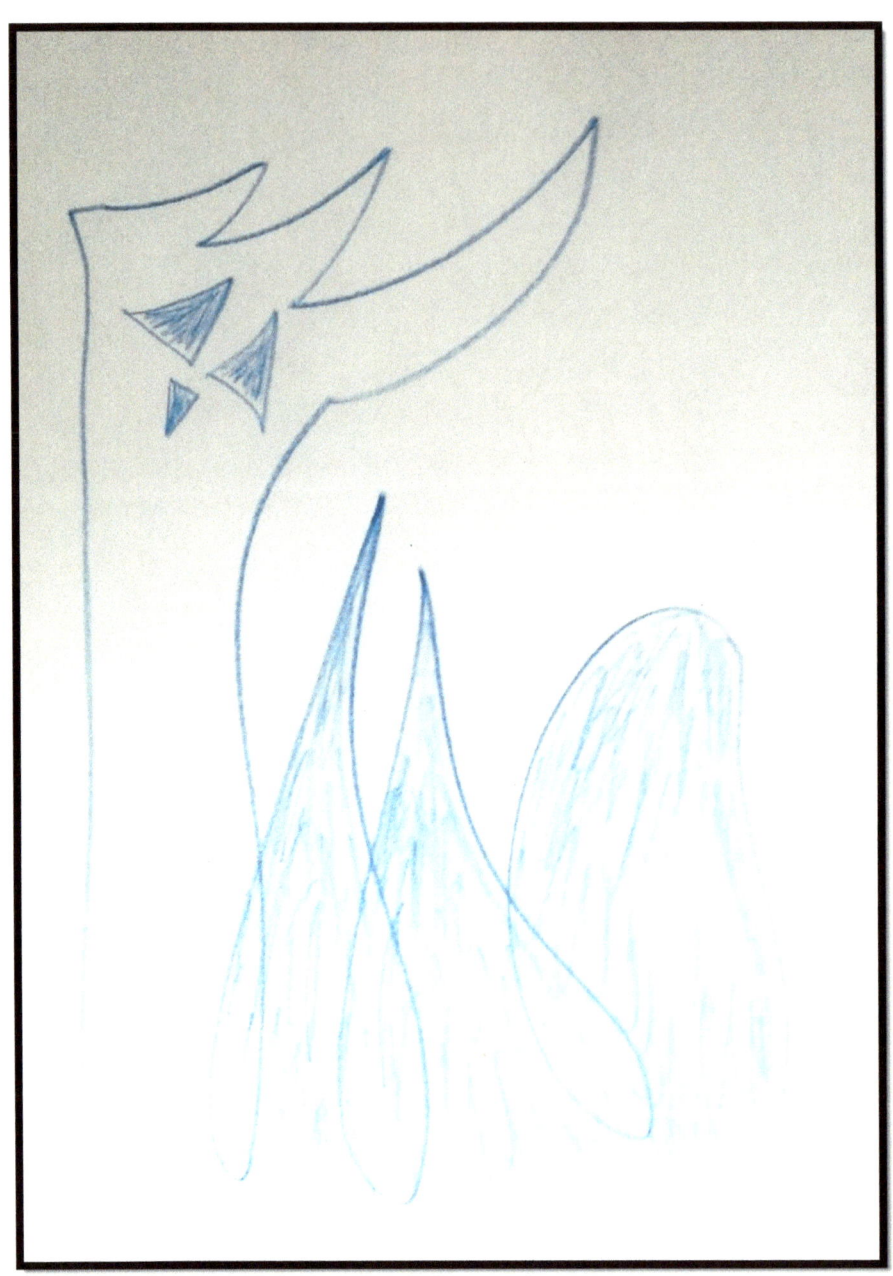

"Water Animal"

"Waving Flag"

It waves to me all the time.

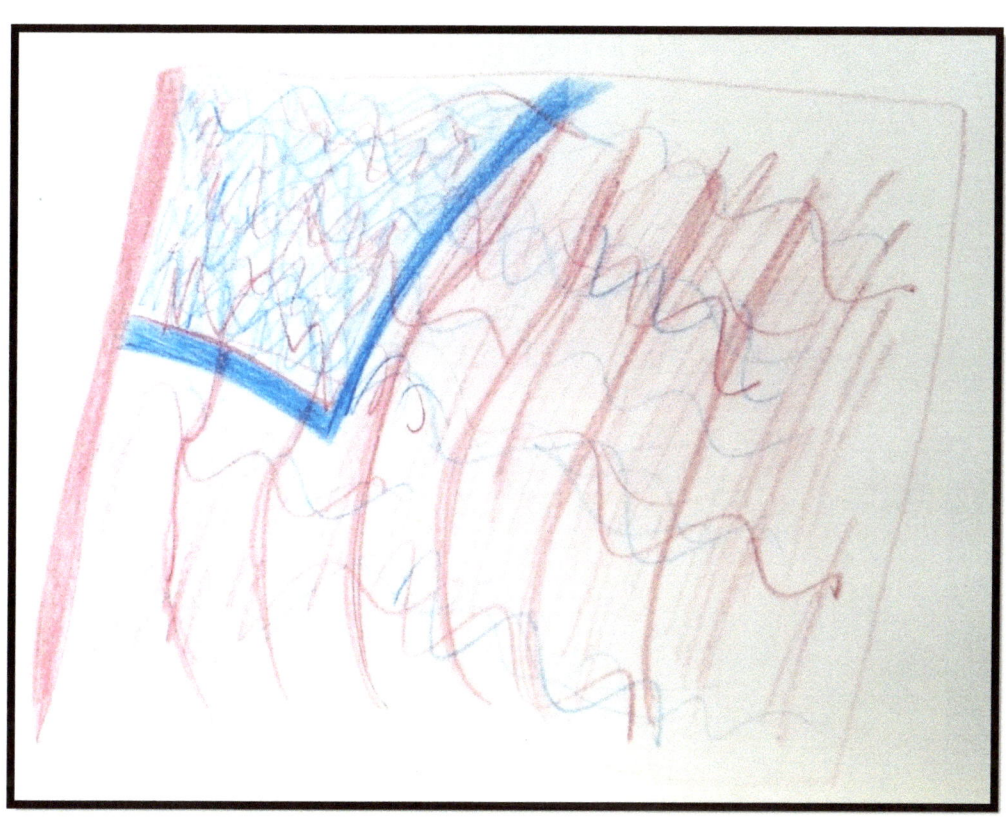

"Another Flag"

I draw a lot of them

I keep on drawing them

So you can remember

What they once stood

4

Not just on the Fourth of July

But Every Day

Of the Year

Every Day

Of the Fear

Every Day

Of the Tear

"A Chapel A Street"

A chapel was on his original street

But then he moved to Chapel Street

He ran through the streets

He ran to the chapel

His story is told in

"Chapel Street Signs"

She says she can hear him

And see his…him too

She wants to help him

Is she creative enough to do it?

Her story is told in

"secret Life OV an antE"

They were meant to fight

To never surrender

That is how it works

With your soul mate

Their story gets told in

"Sri Town"

The series is EcarreT

The story goes on in

"Which of EcarreT"

The series is written in sets

The fifth of the first set is told in

"Hand of Heven"

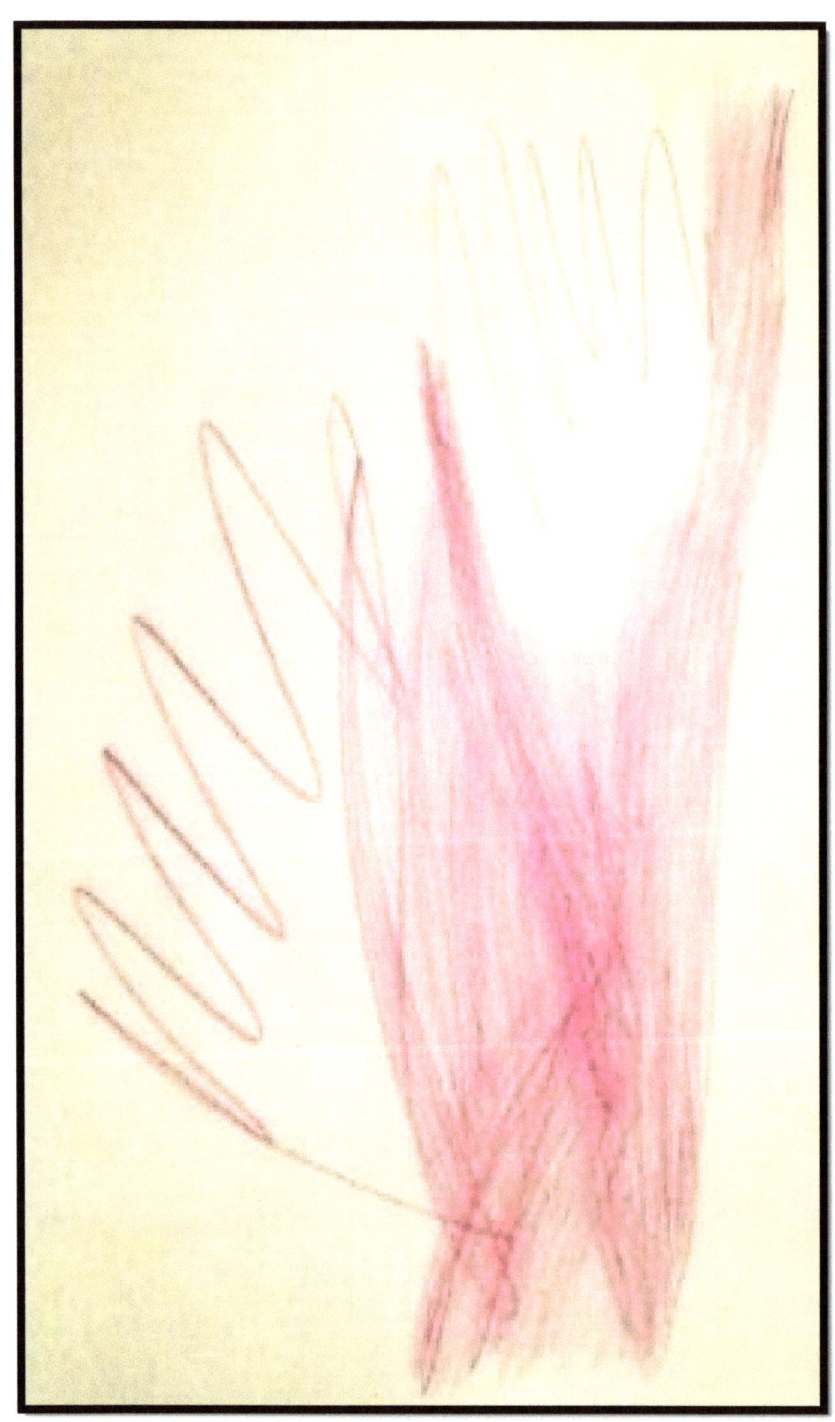

"His Owl"

"Who Who" it would say

Who do you know?

It all depends who you know they would say

I told him I do not know anyone

RL Lane does not know anyone

I just keep going on by myself

Writing and writing

Drawing and drawing

Drew says you never know when books are going to take off

Actually I do know people

But they are already on the other side

Walt and Abner and Thomas Alva and…

Or do I know?

Did they already tell me

When books are going to

Take off.

That rocket. I keep thinking of that rocket.

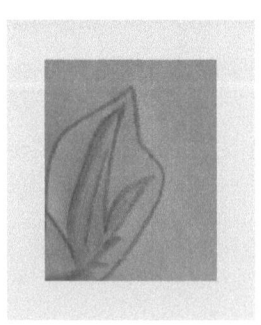

ISBN: 1511974249
ISBN-13: 978-1511974240

www.ingramcontent.com/pod-product-compliance
Lightning Source LLC
Chambersburg PA
CBHW050819180526
45159CB00004B/1720